Engaging with the Sidhe:
Conversations Continued

David Spangler

WORKS BY DAVID SPANGLER

Journey Into Fire
An Introduction to Incarnational Spirituality
Apprenticed to Spirit
Call of the World
Subtle Worlds: *An Explorer's Field Notes*
Working with Subtle Energies
Facing the Future
Blessing: *The Art and the Practice*
The Call
Parent as Mystic—Mystic as Parent
Everyday Miracles
The Laws of Manifestation
Reflections on the Christ
The Story Tree
Starheart and other Stories
The Walker Collection
The Flame of Incarnation
Rhythms and Hues: *Poems of the Beloved*
World Work
Crafting Home: *Generating the Sacred*
Crafting Relationships: *The Holding of Others*
Partnering with Earth
Midsummer's Journey with the Sidhe
The Soul's Oracle (Card Deck)
Manifestation: *Creating the life you love* (Card Deck)
Card Deck of the Sidhe
Conversations with the Sidhe

DEDICATION

I gratefully dedicate this book to all those, Human and Sidhe, who are working for peace, harmony and the wholeness of our world.
Blessing on their efforts

ENGAGING WITH THE SIDHE: CONVERSATIONS CONTINUED

Copyright © 2017 David Spangler

David Spangler has asserted his right to be identified as the author of this work. All rights are reserved, including the right to reproduce this book, or portions thereof, in any form. Reviewers may quote brief passages.

Edited by Julie Spangler and Aidan Spangler

Cover and Interior Design by Jeremy Berg

Published by Lorian Press LLC
Traverse City, Michigan

ISBN: 978-0-936878-96-6

Spangler/David
Engaging with the Sidhe: Conversations Continued/
David Spangler

First Edition April 2017

Printed in the United States of America

0 9 8 7 6 5 4 3 2 1

www.lorian.org

CONTENTS

INTRODUCTION 1
KNOWING MARIEL 5
IMAGINATION 11
NATURE AND THE SIDHE 19
ANWA 23
MARIEL'S WORLD 37
THE "STAR PRIESTESS" 53
MARIEL'S SANCTUARY 60
MARIEL'S CALLING 67
ENGAGING HUMANITY 77
MAKING CONTACT 89
STORIES 96
FINAL THOUGHTS 114

About the Publisher 116

INTRODUCTION

In 2011, I was unexpectedly contacted by a non-physical woman who identified herself as one of the Sidhe (pronounced *shee*), a legendary race of beings known to the ancient Celts and who later were used by J.R.R. Tolkien as models for his elven race in *The Hobbit* and the *Lord of the Rings*. I knew of the Sidhe mainly through my good friend John Matthews who had also contacted these beings some years earlier and had written a book about them called, appropriately enough, *The Sidhe*.

In my own case, the woman who came to me said she was part of a project to encourage and assist more contact between her people and ours. To this end, she presented me with an outline for a set of cards that could be used to facilitate such contact. These particular Sidhe also contacted my colleague and friend, Jeremy Berg, who with their collaboration and help produced a compelling and beautiful set of images to be used with these cards. The result was *The Card Deck of the Sidhe* published by Lorian that same year.

This Sidhe woman who headed up this project had a name I could not pronounce or replicate in English, so she said I could call her "Mariel." My contact with her was not a regular event, but over the next few years, we had several conversations together, most of which were collected and published in 2014 in a book titled *Conversations with the Sidhe*. This book contains much introductory material explaining who Mariel is and the nature of the Sidhe themselves, with whom we humans apparently share an ancient, distant ancestor. I'm not going to repeat all that in this book except where necessary to make clear something Mariel has said. If you are interested, then I refer you to the earlier publication or to the *Card Deck of the Sidhe* itself.

As more people have been using the *Card Deck of the Sidhe* or have read John Matthew's book or mine about the Sidhe, I've gotten many enquiries about what it means to engage with these beings. How can they help us? How can we help them? What does it mean to work with the Sidhe in our daily lives? How can we contact them? And, of course, there is always a curiosity about who they are and how they live.

These are questions that I've had as well. During the years since *Conversations with the Sidhe* was published, I've continued to have contact with Mariel. It's not a steady thing. Sometimes months may go by without any communication between us. When we are in communication, I take the opportunity to ask some of these questions. This book is a compilation of the further conversations we've had on a variety of topics.

Let me say how I communicate with Mariel. Our conversations, for the most part, are not verbal in nature. In my experience, the Sidhe are telepathic but communicate less in words and more in symbols that are packed with meaning, as if they are using mental and emotional hieroglyphs. For me to understand this, we must go beyond telepathy and achieve a blending of spirit and energy fields. This enables me to experience in myself just what it is she is trying to convey as if it were happening to me. This is a direct transmission of meaning. I think of this as a "being-meld" in homage to the "mind-meld" that the Vulcan Spock used in the old Star Trek television series. Mariel also uses words, many plucked, I know, from my own mind, but she doesn't usually assemble them into sentences. Rather she uses them like markers to anchor the meaning she seeks to convey.

Once the communication is finished, I must work out how to translate what has passed between us into words that I can share with others. Therefore, in reading these conversations, you are getting Mariel filtered through me. I do my best to render her thoughts and ideas as clearly and accurately as I can, and I believe I do a good job most of the time as I have many years of experience in doing this kind of translation. But I'm not infallible by any means, and some of the concepts she tries to share are hard to put into human words, even assuming I understand what she's talking about in the first place!

Getting in touch with Mariel is not like ringing up a friend on a phone. Although after many years of contact, I now have her "number," so to speak," getting hold of her is not always guaranteed. She is a busy woman with her own life and duties. While engaging with human beings is something she has chosen to do as a mission, she's not always available. This is especially true if she is in seclusion attuning to the spiritual energies for which she is a conduit.

It has also been my experience that conditions can arise either in our world or in theirs—or in both simultaneously—that can interfere with communication, much like a solar storm can cause static in electromagnetic transmissions here on Earth. There are times when my thoughts and energy can flow gracefully and easily into the Sidhe realm and times when it seems they are blocked or at least must push through turbulence to make a connection. At such times, it may not be worth the energy to try to make that connection, and even if I succeed, I cannot guarantee the clarity or accuracy of the communication because the "being-meld" has not been fully established. Consequently, I may wish to communicate with Mariel, but she may not be able to reciprocate. For this reason, I usually wait for her to contact me, trusting that she has a better sense of when conditions are right for such a contact than I may have.

The Sidhe world is diverse. When I ask Mariel questions about the Sidhe, it's as if I were asking an American to discourse about the nature of humanity. Certainly, Americans share various characteristics in common with other humans, but American culture is very different from that of Japan, China, Venezuela or Nigeria. What may be true for a North American may not at all be true for someone living in Zambia or Nepal. Mariel is not a spokesperson for all the Sidhe. As Mariel herself points out, she mainly speaks for those Sidhe with whom she is familiar and who work with her.

Knowing someone is a lifetime proposition. I've known my wife Julia for forty-six years, and I'm happily still discovering new things about her that enrich and deepen our relationship. I expect I will never stop learning who Julia is, and part of this process is one of, when necessary, discarding the mental images I form about her. For each of us is more than any image can encompass. This is particularly true of the Sidhe. The moment I think I know who they are or who Mariel is, something comes along that shows how little I do know and how much I still must learn.

This is why I consider the material in my previous book and in this one as "field notes" in an evolving study and exploration. Everything I share with you is based on my experiences but also on my interpretation of things at any given point in my study. Nothing should be taken as a "final revelation" about the Sidhe. Given the differences that can exist between individual Sidhe and groups of Sidhe, your experience of them might not be the same as my own. If I were a visitor from outer space and I landed in China, I would be wrong to base my understanding of humanity only on my encounter with a few Chinese. I might miss entirely the reality of other races, other cultures, other ways of being that make humanity such a complex and diverse species.

The following conversations occurred at different times over a period of three years, increasing in frequency as I began working on this book and had questions to ask. I've not attempted to arrange this material chronologically. Sometimes Mariel would say something and then two months or more later would provide introductory material that put what she had said before in a clearer context. What I've done is arrange my notes of our conversations in thematic order to enhance their clarity. Some ideas naturally precede others. I present them here in that way even though I may have received the information from Mariel in a different sequence as our conversations unfolded between us.

KNOWING MARIEL

Being able to engage with the Sidhe depends on understanding them. Certainly, this has been true for me. It's not simply a cognitive understanding, knowing several facts about them. It's an understanding of the heart. I usually call this understanding a *felt sense*, and it's something that's held in the entire body, not just the mind but not excluding the mind, either. It probably comes close to understanding what Mariel calls *anwa*. I'll have much more to say about this later. Mariel defines it as a quality that arises from within a being as an expression of who they are in relationship to their environment. It's a kind of "identity-through-action" or as she puts it, "spirit in motion."

Having this kind of understanding facilitates attunement and enhances collaboration. But it's not easy to come by. At least, it has not been for me.

I want to share what this process has been like for me as a way of opening the discussions and conversations of this book. In so doing, I want to emphasize that understanding Mariel—much less the Sidhe as a whole--is still a work in progress.

When Mariel first appeared, I had no idea at first just who or even what she was. I have had over sixty years of experience of sensing subtle world energies and beings, but this first encounter with the Sidhe was different from anything I had ever experienced before. The felt sense of what was impacting my energy field or aura was new. My first thought was, is this a subtle being? If not, what is this?

I had been sitting on a sofa at the time, facing the living room. Behind me was a large picture window that looks out over our front yard, the main street of our neighborhood. and neighbors' houses beyond. Part of this view is obscured by branches from a cluster of Douglas Fir trees that form part of a boundary between our property and that of the family next door. The burst of energy and swirling Light that I felt and saw seemed to come from the middle of this group of trees which led me at first to wonder if it was some manifestation of nature spirits associated with them. However, I'm reasonably familiar with the felt sense of many of the nature spirits that inhabit our yard. A quick moment's reflection convinced me that whatever this visitation was, it was not from one of the tree spirits. Much later, Mariel told me that she used the energy of these trees as a conduit or as a kind of portal from her world into mine.

What I saw at first was a cloud of Light within which energies were swirling. As I focused my subtle senses upon it, I could discern a pale face in the middle of this swirl. There was no body, not even a full head, just a face with sharp, angular features and piercing black eyes with a gaze that was forceful and commanding. There was something inhuman, almost feral about this face. What I most felt in that first contact was Mariel's will to make a connection. In subsequent encounters, her features have softened, but the initial impression they conveyed was of an intensity pulling everything towards a point of focus to contact me.

I could not tell at first if this face were that of a male or female and thought it might be androgynous. As it turned out, there were two male Sidhe who accompanied Mariel on this first contact. Initially, their energies blended together in this swirling Light to create this sense of androgyny, but as the connection stabilized and clarified itself, I could distinguish between the three of them. At that point, the strong feminine presence made itself known, and I knew that my primary contact was with a woman.

I knew about the Sidhe, both from reading legends and lore of the ancient Celts and from John Matthews' excellent book on the subject, *The Sidhe*. I never actually expected to run into any of them. It seemed to me, without giving the matter much thought, that they were an exotic mystery that belonged half a world away. I was astonished, therefore, when the woman identified herself and her companions as Sidhe. She said that if I were willing, they would like to do a project with me. I said yes, I was willing, and without hesitation, as soon as I said this, my mind was filled with a complete description of what became the *Card Deck of the Sidhe*, what its elements were, how it was to be used, and why the Sidhe were offering it as a means of connection with their world. The whole process probably took under a minute. As soon as Mariel knew that I had grasped what she was presenting and would remember it, the three of them vanished. The whole encounter did not last much more than five minutes, if even that long.

I was excited by what I had received. Jeremy Berg, as publisher of Lorian Press, had asked me some weeks earlier if I could design a card deck about the Sidhe. I had declined because I knew virtually nothing about them and had no inner sense of them upon which to draw. Now, thanks to this contact, I had a clear vision of just how to proceed. I immediately phoned Jeremy to tell him the good news.

However, all this was tempered by uneasiness. Frankly, I was intimidated by what I had felt with Mariel. I felt the strength of her will. I also felt danger as well, such as I might feel in the presence of a wild animal. She felt wild, feral, fierce, powerful, unpredictable, and altogether non-human. For some reason, it was precisely these qualities that convinced me that she was what she said she was, a Sidhe, a presence to be reckoned with. I was grateful for the gift of inspiration about the card deck, but I felt some trepidation about continuing the contact.

The project of the card deck, however, served as a meeting ground for us. It created an atmosphere of collaboration which in turn allowed us a chance to get to know each other better. I have already said that the means of communication that I use is one of a blending of energy fields. It's an intimate process, a "being-meld" that goes beyond telepathy. The challenge was that my energy field was accustomed to engaging and blending with beings and intelligences inhabiting the non-physical subtle realms. Over seventy years of doing this, my subtle field was configured for this kind of attunement. It's as if my subtle field is a receiver for FM radio broadcasts. However, when I experience contact with the Sidhe, it's as if they are "broadcasting" using microwaves rather than radio waves. So, to work with the Sidhe, I must adjust my energy field to act more like a cell phone than a radio receiver.

It's important to realize, though, that the Sidhe are not subtle beings. They are as physical as you and I, but they inhabit an aspect of the physical world where matter is less material. Mariel was very clear on this point.

> **MARIEL**: I am not a spirit. I have a soul as you do, and I have a body. My body, like yours, is made of matter, but the matter of my world is less formed, less conditioned, than yours. It is more primal and fluid. You would probably say it is less like matter and more like energy, but these are two different states of one thing. We occupy one level of that one thing, and you occupy another.

It's as if our world is made of ice and theirs is made of water or even of water vapor, but both worlds are still manifestations of H^2O.

Working together on the card deck meant that Mariel would come to give advice and perspective several times a month at the beginning of the project. This gave me plenty of practice in aligning with her. As I did so, I realized that some of the difficult energy and danger I'd been feeling was due to the inability of my energy field to fully blend with hers at first. As this changed and our connection became more graceful and attuned, more of her personality came to the fore. As it did so, I lost my trepidation. I realized that she was a very loving, joyful, and compassionate individual. She lost none of her power or fierceness, but I could experience these qualities in the larger context of her whole being.

Initially, I saw Mariel as a shimmering field of energy and Light within which was a face. As we became acquainted, the features of the face softened as I grew more aware of her loving nature. This was also a reflection of the fact that she did not have to use so much intensity of will to enter the subtle environment of the earth to contact me. Greater familiarity with her energy and greater facility in making my energy field behave like a "cell phone" meant that we each had to do less work to engage and communicate. This allowed more of her nature to communicate itself to my consciousness.

As the contact continued and deepened, I realized that I was increasingly seeing her as a woman and not as a powerful but formless energy field. Over time, this feminine figure became more human in appearance as well. As this happened, Mariel said, "You are creating a thought-form of me drawing on the humanness we share from our ancient common source. This is helpful, as it makes it easier for your mind to connect with me." This continued for some months, although once the card deck was published, our contacts became less frequent.

Contact picked up again when I began working on *Conversations with the Sidhe*. Once again, my image of her as a woman helped. Mariel had become a very real person to me. There came a time, though, when I noticed it was becoming harder rather than easier to have a clear communication with her. I asked Mariel about this, and she said, "Be careful. Your image of me is becoming too human and replacing who I really am. It is interfering with our connection."

To correct this, I had to go all the way back to our first few contacts and recapture the sense of wildness and non-humanness that I had felt then. This time, though, I could go beyond these initial impressions.

The Sidhe are often associated with nature and are even confused with being nature spirits. There is no question they are deeply attuned to Gaia and to the natural world, but they are not wild. At least, Mariel and her colleagues are not. What had seemed like wildness to me was, I realized, the way my mind interpreted her non-humanness. It was something else as well.

As I've come to know the Sidhe through Mariel and through occasional contact with her associates and colleagues, I realize who they are is shaped by the land which they occupy. This forms part of their *anwa*, as we shall see later. They are beings who embody the ecology of which they are a part. They are connected to their world in ways that are latent if not atrophied in ourselves. Consequently, when I contact a Sidhe like Mariel, I am also contacting her world. She comes to me carrying the energy and presence of her world and her connections with it. I realized upon reflection that it was the presence of these connections that I had also interpreted as "wildness." I had had a sense of Mariel belonging to wilderness rather than to "civilization." This was inaccurate, as I later found out. This characteristic of being an embodiment of an ecosystem has nothing to do with nature in the way we tend to think of it and everything to do with being deeply integrated into the life of their whole world.

As I began to appreciate this, Mariel "filled out," so to speak, taking on more substance for me because I was now perceiving her in a more holistic way.

During our first encounters, I realized that Mariel was a being of power. There was a short time in the first two or three encounters when I wondered if she might be the Queen of the Sidhe, the so-called "Faerie Queen," as there was such an aura of authority about her. As she said in *Conversations with the Sidhe*, this was an incorrect perception on my part, born in part from the fact that she had been overlighted and assisted in contacting me by an elder Sidhe Presence who was highly evolved and in some ways, like a Sidhe Queen.

What was evident to me was that Mariel was a woman of spiritual power as evidenced by the Light I felt around her and flowing through her. She was like a shaman or a priestess; indeed, I began thinking of her as a priestess. Like the image of her as a human woman, she allowed me to have this idea for a time, and it influenced how I translated the images and impressions that flowed from her. Indeed, I couldn't find a word or concept that quite fit who she is and the role she plays; "priestess" came the closest. So I used this term to describe her—I even went further and called her a "star-priestess" because of the quality of subtle energies I felt around her. She agreed to it as a place to start. Certainly, it was the image in my mind when I was working on the previous book of communications. But eventually, like the image of her as a human woman, it, too, became an impediment to our contact.

If nothing else, I have learned again just how easy it is for us to form images about these people that then crystallize and take on a greater reality for us than they should. It's like having a radio that allows us to hear a distant voice and then beginning to identify the radio *as* that voice. Our imagination and the images and thought-forms it generates can be wonderful instruments of bridging our consciousness to worlds and realms outside of the incarnate human experience; they are just the bridge, however, and not that which crosses over it.

IMAGINATION

My way of meeting Mariel and getting to know her is facilitated by the faculty of imagination. This doesn't mean that she is "imaginary." It does mean that she and I jointly use images in my mind as points of connection that can expand into a deeper communion of sharing and knowing. In this process, as I have come to know Mariel, I've gained an expanded understanding of imagination itself, including the different ways that she and I see and experience it. Since it is such an important tool, I felt discussing it would be an important way to begin the field notes of our conversations.

We think of imagination as a capacity to form mental images. Most people probably think of it as an ability to "make things up." If something is imaginary, it's not real. Certainly, we can make up images that have no basis in reality. In a broader sense, we may see it as a creative ability. Certainly, everything that we have in our human world originated either in its form or in its application in someone's imagination. Someone thought up the cell phone and the automobile. For that matter, someone saw fire in nature and imagined its usefulness as a source of energy.

In esoteric lore and teaching, imagination is not simply a creative tool, though it certainly is that, but also one of perception. We see through our imaginations. In a way, this is true of physical perception as well, for our brain constructs the image of the world that we perceive out of the electromagnetic and biochemical impulses that come to it from the environment. In an analogous way, subtle energies I may encounter in the non-physical environment also translate themselves into images in my mind through the imaginative function. How accurate these images are depends on a number of factors but among them are the clarity, openness, and flexibility of my imagination.

For Mariel, though, imagination is not solely a private mental activity but a way of describing part of the substance and fabric of the world. Here is what she has said about this.

MARIEL: For you, imagination is a subjective experience. For us it is objective. It is a quality of fluidity and responsiveness within the life of the matter that forms the substance of our world. It is why our world is so directly responsive to our thoughts. In a way, you might say that we live in imagination.

This is true for you, too, but it is not so obvious because of the solidity of your world. Thought crystallizes more densely in your version of the physical dimension. Imagination bifurcates into what is within you and what is outside you.

DAVID: It seems to me you are speaking of imagination as a substance rather than as a function.

MARIEL: Are you so sure these are two separate things? In your world, yes, they manifest that way. In my world, less so. In the realms of consciousness in which the Earth Soul operates—the one you call Gaia—hardly at all.

For us, imagination refers to a primal quality of matter. Think of it as grace within matter, the protean power to respond to creative will. It is a fluidity of being. When I imagine, I am engaging with this living, responsive presence within matter. But imagination is more than a function. What you experience as imagination is matter blending with the impulse of a thought and forming itself accordingly. You see it as a psychological function because you do not see the subtle forces at work taking on the shapes of what you are thinking. Imagination is the quality of matter that allows shape-shifting to occur.

For you, imagination is an internal experience. For us, it is the substance of the world we live in. Let me see if I can make this clearer to you with this metaphor. Physical life began in the ancient oceans of the world. When life left the ocean and began to dwell upon the land, it carried that ocean within it in its blood stream. You still have the ancient ocean within you. But other forms of life remained in the ocean and are in direct, outer contact with its watery environment.

Imagination is like the ancient ocean. Through your incarnational processes, you have entered the "land" of a dense, physical world, but you carry this ancient ocean of imagination, this fluidity of substance, within you. Your personal energy field is living matter that is responsive to your thoughts and feelings. It shapes itself in part according to your psychological life. Your physical surroundings, though, are less responsive and in some instances, not responsive at all to your inner projections. We, however, are like the fish that never left the sea. We swim in that ancient ocean of living matter, and it flows through us.

This is partly why you experience us as possessing what you call glamour. You are experiencing in us the call of the ancient ocean from which you yourselves arise. I mean this metaphorically, but in fact, you feel in us a magic that you once possessed but which is now held for the most part within your subjective life. For you, we are imagination given flesh. I do not mean that we are imaginary or made up, though you can certainly create thought-forms of us. I mean that we embody the substance that is imagination. It is as if you are ice remembering what it is like to be flowing water, and when you encounter us, we are that water taken form.

This generates glamor for you, as I said. It can heighten the presence of imagination within you, both psychologically and as a substance. Some of us make use of this glamor deliberately to affect your people, sometimes in sport, sometimes to teach you lessons, sometimes, I am sad to say, with ill intent and even selfishness on our part. We are not perfect either!

We do not possess imagination individually as much as we participate in the "ocean of imagination" that is part of the life of the world. This does not mean that we cannot form images or imagine new forms as you do, but we do so in collaboration with the flow of imagination within the world. This is why it is very easy for us to manifest in form and substance what we think about, an ability that seems like magic to you. But your ability to fashion a complete world in your imagination seems like magic to us. Do you understand? It's as if you have your own private inner ocean that you can populate with life of your choosing. We do not have this. We work magic in our outer lives; you work it in your inner lives.

Of course, this carries risks for you, for you can populate your ocean with predatory fish that attack you more than others. The thought-forms you create impact you powerfully and shape your personal world. You can bind yourself with your thoughts and images in ways that would be difficult for us to duplicate, and you can liberate and attune yourselves to the world in ways that we cannot.

When you bring your ancient inner ocean of imagination—of living matter—into synchronization and harmony with the imagination of the world, then you can have a powerful effect. You can bless the world in ways beyond our ability. But you can curse it as well. This is your incarnate challenge as human beings.

Here is where we feel our collaboration can be helpful, for we can help receive and channel your imaginative powers in ways that are more harmonious with the life of Gaia. Your inner magic can emerge to harmonize with the magic in the world with which we are familiar. This possibility is what lies behind our project of exploring collaboration with you.

During a later contact, Mariel came back to this issue of imagination in the context of discussing the history of our two branches of humanity.

MARIEL: As you know, we were once one people. We share a common ancestry in spirit. When we came to this world, long before there were humans or Sidhe, it was in part to learn how to work with the creative impulses that were forming this planet. In a way, we became stewards and students of Gaia's imagination. By this I mean of Gaia's creative relationship to the living spirit of matter from which the planet was shaped.

When we split, a result was that you carried this learning and stewardship into the private laboratory of your own energy field and incarnate consciousness. You were like a scientist who wished to isolate a phenomenon to study it more closely. As a consequence, what you experience as your personal imagination came into being, allowing you the challenge and the privilege of creating your own inner world. You will remember that I said it was as if you had filled yourself with a portion of the ancient ocean of the consciousness of living matter. We, on the other hand, remained in touch with the imagination of the world and continued to be its stewards and students.

All boundaries are permeable, so we could say that your private ocean of imagination leaked and formed a collective sea to which all humans have access and which therefore affects all humans. You would call this the collective imagination of your race, and it has shaped for itself a domain, an imaginal world, within the greater life and imagination of Gaia.

If your personal imagination is your soul's personal laboratory for the study of the life and responsiveness of matter, then this imaginal world is humanity's collective laboratory to do the same thing. And here, both individually and collectively, you are learning how to master the relationships that draw this life of matter into partnership and harmony with you.

I put it this way because you are influenced by the idea of mind over matter and of using your imagination as a tool rather than as a partner. But imagination is a relationship. We see it as the gracefulness of matter that allows it to mold itself in partnership. It is a way of being in the world and with the world that draws out and enhances the life within matter. You are learning this in a most intimate and personal way which ultimately will give you much wisdom and power in the love you bring to the life of the world.

Here is a way to think about this. Every day through your thinking and feeling, you are shaping your inner world. If your private world were to become a collective world—if your imagination became the imagination of the world, and the world reflected the quality and direction of your thoughts and feelings—what kind of world would you be living in?

In effect, this happens already, for as I said, your inner world leaks constantly into the pool of imagination you all share, thus shaping the human world you experience.

You are learning about the nature and power of imagination in ways that we cannot, for we do not have private laboratories in the same sense that you do. But we swim in the larger ocean of which your private sea is only a puddle. This does not make us more powerful, but it makes us more connected. It's this connection that you lack. It's why your personal and collective thought-forms can be so destructive.

When you take an animal into the laboratory, you can study it and learn a great deal about its constitution. But what you will not learn is how it lives in its own habitat. You will not learn how it is part of its ecosystem. For that, you must live with the animal in the wild to learn how it is connected. You are dissecting and analyzing imagination and learning how it functions, but what you are not learning is how it is connected. We are the ecologists of imagination; we know what it is in its natural habitat. We live with it in the wild, whereas you live with it in the laboratory of your minds. If we pool our wisdom and insights together, we will be better able to fulfill the ancient mission of our common ancestor to understand and to steward the imagination of the world.

When Mariel began working on the *Card Deck of the Sidhe* with Jeremy and me, she and her associates specified clearly that there should be no attempt to portray the Sidhe in the cards. "You may suggest our presence and our qualities," she said, "but do not create any images of us." When I asked her why, she said, "We do not wish to fetter your imagination of who we are, but likewise we do not wish to be fettered by your images."

In one of her first conversations with me, Mariel had said that while she was solid in her own realm, the closer she came to my world, the "wispier" she got, such that her shape could be influenced by human thought-forms. In the light of the communication I just reported, this made sense. She and her colleagues—and perhaps the Sidhe as a whole—are sensitive to the currents and influences of imagination. In her own world, she is in partnership with these currents in ways that support and solidify her chosen form, but when she comes into our world, the very sensitivity that makes this partnership possible also makes her vulnerable to be shaped by the power of our personal and collective imaginations. This is what was happening when my imagination of her became more and more human, as I described. It reached a point where it interfered rather than helped the contact. As she said, "The less you imagine us, the more able we are to imagine ourselves in your consciousness."

Because of these conversations, I asked Mariel what advice she or another Sidhe might offer about how we as incarnate humans, their cousins, might better use our imaginations. Here is her reply.

MARIEL: Because of the differences between us, my reflections may not be of as much value as those given by another of your kind. For you, imagination is something you do. For us, it is something you are. Yes, you use your imaginations to create unreal worlds for yourselves, but you should not define the nature of imagination by this alone. It is not simply a means for making things up or even for creative endeavor.

You live in a world that you perceive as containing subjects and objects, those who act and those who are acted upon. My world contains only subjects; I think in terms of acting with rather than acting upon. For this reason, imagination to me is an experience of relationship. Imagination connects me to my world and its potentials.

As I see it, imagination also connects you, but in your case, it connects you as well to yourself and to your own potentials, to your inner world. For this reason, your imagination has a more powerful effect upon you than mine does upon me. I am aware, you see, of how I exist in the imagination of Gaia, and my imagination works outward from me to be in relationship and harmony with this. My self-image is a collaborative one, worked out in the relationship between my identity and the identity of the world. All this is contained for me in the concept of *anwa*.

Your imagination, however, works inward upon you, and the effects of this flow outward into the world. Where I am *part* of a world, *part* of a flow of imagination through the world, you *are* a world, shaped by your thoughts and feelings. You can imagine yourself as an independent actor in the world in ways that are foreign to me, even though I have a strong sense of my identity. While I am free to make choices, I am influenced, though not compelled, by what flows through me and connects me to my world.

This is a power, my friend; it's a power to shape your outer world, certainly, but even more it is a power to shape yourselves for better or for worse. Therefore, if I have advice to give, it is first to be aware of how you are using this power. How are you imagining yourself? What inner world are you creating that then impresses itself upon the fluid matrix of the world around you? Second, use your imagination to connect. Use it to enter the inner worlds of others different from your own so that communion, connection, and understanding can build between you. Use your imagination to love.

Beyond this, it's not for me to say. You are in a different

evolutionary condition than I am. You face different challenges and have different gifts and talents with which to meet them than I do. I am like a sea creature to your land animal, a creature of the ocean speaking to one who carries the ocean around inside him. We both share this ocean; it is essential to our lives, but we engage with it differently. How may the sea creature advise the one who lives on land?

The idea that we live in the world of our imagination more than we live in the unifying experience of the world's imagination is an important one. Our imagination gives us uniqueness as we each imagine who we are in the world in our own way. But this very ability can divide us from each other, something we are seeing played out in political and social ways right now (not that there's anything new to such divisions!). The counterbalance is to use our imagination to see beyond our own boundaries and beliefs; we talk about this as "walking in another's shoes" or "seeing from another's perspective." The point is simply that our powers of imagination can build barriers or build bridges between us. We may feel the Sidhe have an advantage over us because of their innate sense of unity together, but the human experience teaches us how to be bridge-builders, something the Sidhe do not learn in the same way.

NATURE AND THE SIDHE

One of the most common ways of imagining the Sidhe is to see them as creatures of nature, perhaps even as nature spirits. There is no question that many Sidhe, if not all, have a deep attunement to nature, though one might clarify this to say that what they have is a deep attunement to life, interconnectedness, and wholeness. I felt it important to address this image right off the bat and allow Mariel to comment on this common perception.

>   **MARIEL**: Let me ask, are *you* a nature spirit? So much depends on perception and definition. There are many humans who are deeply attuned to nature, so much so that their presence is nourishing and empowering to the natural life around them. Are they nature spirits? Not by origin, certainly, but they are by function, are they not?
>   Be careful of the categories you create unless you end up chopping the world into smaller and smaller segments. It is good to make distinctions that aid your understanding, but do so mindfully and with an awareness that life itself is not always bound to those distinctions.
>   The Sidhe are indeed attuned to nature and draw upon its forces for our well-being in addition to offering what we can to the well-being of the world. "Nature," of course, is more than just what you see with your physical senses. Often, the "nature" to which we are attuned is on a higher frequency of life than what you find in your physical world. The true nature spirits work with the physical embodiments of life. These are the incarnations of creative impulses coming from what you term the Devic and angelic realms. There are Sidhe who assist with this as well, just as you have human gardeners who plunge their hands into the soil to plant and tend their seeds. But most Sidhe are attuned to a different level of manifestation.
>   Consider that "nature" is simply the presence of life in your world; as custodians of life, of course we have our connections to this presence.

I've had contact with nature spirits of various kinds for as long as I can remember. They have been part of the environment for me, part of the background. *Nature spirit* is one of those umbrella terms that covers a universe of distinct manifestations. What all such beings have in common is that they are part of the circulation of living energies between Gaia, the physical realm, and in some cases, the solar and cosmic realms. One of the things I have learned is that subtle energies are almost always mediated or channeled by beings of one kind or another. The image that comes to mind, though it's hardly exact, is that of a red blood cell that carries life-giving food and energy to the cells of the body. So, for instance, I'm aware of the nature spirits that attend to the maple tree in my backyard and can perceive how they receive subtle life energies from higher vibrational levels and "fix" them, much like the bacteria that "fix" free nitrogen in the air into the soil where it can be absorbed by the roots of plants. These energies become part of the "body" or field of these nature beings in a way that the energy body of the physical tree can access and absorb them.

The topic of nature spirits is one that could fill a book. But there is one category of nature being that seems to me to occupy a distinct and special niche in the energy ecology of Gaia. These are the ones we call "fairies" or as they are called in many esoteric traditions, the Faerie beings. I have not had as much contact with these beings as I have with those I think of as nature spirits, but from what I have observed, it seems to me that the Faerie beings are individuated nature spirits, operating with a more complex and autonomous consciousness and will than the kind of nature spirits I feel around my maple tree, for instance.

One experience that stands out for me of contact with a member of the Faerie realm occurred when I was attending an event at a conference center in West Seattle. This center was built on a hill overlooking Puget Sound and the Olympic Mountain range to the west. There was a broad lawn between the main building of the center and the edge of the hill; walking on the paths that criss-crossed this lawn was a pleasure as the view was spectacular.

During an afternoon break, I went out to enjoy the view and to take a walk around the grounds. The path I was on wound towards the edge of the lawn where there was a line of trees. As I walked along, my thoughts focused on the snow-capped mountains off in the distance, I realized I was feeling uneasy. I seemed to be entering an unwelcoming patch of energy, which brought my attention back to the path and the lawn around me and also heightened my subtle senses. There was nothing about the area of the lawn I was walking towards that stood out as being different or unusual to my physical senses, but inwardly I could perceive that something was there, though I couldn't make out what it was.

I took a few more steps along the path, and suddenly found myself confronted by a being about three feet or so in height, looking quite human except for pointed ears and dressed in slacks and a tunic. "Please do not come any further," he said. His tone was polite and friendly enough, but I sensed behind his words a strong will that I pay attention and turn back. I realized I was talking to a Faerie being, an elf to be precise, and I could feel, not a sense of danger exactly but a warning. Of course, the polite thing to do was to turn around and leave that stretch of lawn alone, which is what I did. I have no idea what was going on or whether I could have been harmed in any way had I chosen to ignore this being, but the elf had asked nicely for my cooperation, and I had no reason not to give it.

There is a great deal of folklore and tradition around the Faerie Realms and Faerie beings, and often these stories overlap and blend with stories of the Sidhe so that it can be difficult to distinguish between them. I think it's not uncommon to confuse the two, but in my experience at least, they are two different species. For one thing, the Sidhe share a common ancestor with humanity, so in part at least, they have human qualities. Faerie beings such as elves, gnomes, kobolds, dryads, and the like, are wholly non-human and do not have a common ancestor with us or with the Sidhe. They are, as Mariel calls them, the "Children of Gaia."

It is evident to me that the Faerie beings are among those Mariel calls the "intermediaries." I felt it worth asking her about this and how she sees the distinction between herself and her people and the Faeries.

> **MARIEL**: You ask about the Faerie people. You are correct in perceiving that they are not who we are. However, the line between us can be blurry, for there are those Sidhe who work closely with the Faerie Folk just as I work with you; as I take on more human semblance for our association, so those who work with the realms of Faerie take on Faerie form. And the reverse is true, for Faeries are shape-changers as much as we who can, as you know, appear in human form or in Sidhe form if it pleases them to do so.

The Faerie Folk are incarnations within the life-field and body of Gaia, even as you and I are. But where Sidhe and Human have their origin within the stellar realms, the Faerie Folk are born out of Gaia. They are truly Gaia's children, whereas we are children of the stars who are for a time integral parts of Gaia's being.

The beings you perceive as nature spirits may be Faerie, but they may also be manifestations of Gaia's life itself. These are beings who are not incarnated in the way you and I are—or the way that many of the Faerie Folk are; they do not have a separate existence apart from Gaia. They are truly like the cells in Gaia's energy body. But Faerie Folk have greater independence and are an evolutionary line in their own right. If a nature spirit that is part of Gaia's body should seek to evolve into its own independent life, it will most likely do so by becoming part of the Faerie realm. Where they meet, the boundary between the Faerie Folk and nature spirits is permeable and diffuse, with beings shifting back and forth. At this level, it can be difficult to say which is which. But as evolution takes place, the Faerie Folk, though always deeply embedded in and attuned to the life of nature, become more independent and individualized, though they always retain elements of a collective consciousness.

The Faerie Folk are our allies and companions. Many Sidhe work closely and exclusively with them. I am not one of them. My calling is elsewhere, as you know. But for those Sidhe who have entered the Faerie realm in communion and collaboration, it can be difficult for a human to tell them apart.

ANWA

In my communications with Mariel and her colleagues over the years, *anwa* has been a central concept, something to which they refer again and again. Understanding it is important to understanding the Sidhe themselves, at least as important as understanding the use of imagination. What is *anwa*? Here is how Mariel described it in a conversation some years ago:

> **MARIEL**: The true shape of anything isn't what it looks like but what it is as an activity of life. You do not have a word for this. It is something's function, yes, but also how life moves and flows within and around it, and the intentionality that powers that movement. You might use a word like "spirit" but it is not truly the spirit of something. Rather it is the moving pattern that the spirit imparts. We call this the *anwa*.
>
> If we see a tree, we are aware of the spirit of the tree and also of its form, its trunk and branches, how its roots go into the earth, the shape of its leaves, and so forth. The *anwa* stands between these two things. It is the shape of the tree's spirit's intent and the activity and functions that flow from that intent.

The Sidhe are deeply sensitive to the *anwa* of all living things—which from their point of view includes everything—and this includes the *anwa* of the planet itself. The non-physical beings known as Devas and nature spirits are intrinsically part of the subtle energetic metabolism of Gaia. The Sidhe are not, but they can be allies that help that metabolism in its planetary functioning. They do so through their ability to sense and work with the *anwa* of a plant or animal, a landscape or ecosystem, or of the world.

Knowing the importance of this concept, I asked Mariel if she could explain it more fully.

> **MARIEL**: *Anwa* is not the same as spirit or soul, though they are related. *Anwa* emerges from the intent of a soul or spirit—its will to be a certain thing in a certain way—so it reflects the innate identity of that soul or spirit. But it is the motion of that intent and identity as it encounters the whole environment in which it is

manifesting. *Anwa* is like the pattern of a dance, and in a dance, there are always partners. *Anwa* emerges out of connection and collaboration and reflects the movement that partners create in their dancing.

When we see a tree, for instance, its *anwa* is not just the identity and pattern of that tree as an individual expression of its species. It is also the relationships it is forming with the soil, with the air, with other plants in its vicinity, with the animals that may feed on its fruits, if any, and with the birds that nest in its branches. *Anwa* reflects the potentials that these characteristics make possible.

DAVID: What I think of as you describe *anwa* is that it represents the dynamic, energetic shape of the "coming-into-being" of an entity, whatever or whoever it is, and this shape is always subject to change within a particular set of parameters. In other words, the tree you mention—let's use the maple tree in my backyard as an example—its *anwa* is both its "maple-ness" and its relationship with the land from which it is growing, with me and my family, with our house, with other trees in our backyard and the neighbors' yards, with the influence of the nearby lake and mountains, and so on. The maple tree comes into being as a unique individual tree as a product of all these relationships.

MARIEL: Yes, I understand what you are thinking and I would agree, though I would say that the *anwa* of your maple tree is not simply the relationships it forms but how it forms them. It is how it engages, not simply that it engages. Let me give you another example. Let us say you have a source of water, and from this source, water is going to flow down into the land. As you study the land, you can see the route the water is likely to take based on how the land is formed. The *anwa* of the water is both its source of water and the channels that will most likely define its pattern of flow.

DAVID: You're saying that *anwa* is a kind of inner topology that represents not only what is there but what could be there, the "paths of least resistance," so to speak.

MARIEL: In a matter of speaking, yes. Imagine now the water is flowing into the land. It flows into the channels that represent the paths of least resistance, as you call them, but as it flows, it alters those channels and may create new ones that were unanticipated. Do you see? *Anwa* is not only shaped by the influence of the environment but also by the influence it can bring to bear upon the environment, which thereby changes it. When we see the *anwa* of something, we see this potential.

Be careful with the words you choose, though, for *anwa* is not seen in the same way you might see the energy field around a being. It is not an aura. You think about *anwa*, and you try to find words to express and define it. I understand why you do this, especially if you are to share this concept with others. But this is not how I experience *anwa*. I do not think into it or about it. I feel into it as an extension of my body. You could say I see it with my heart...no, with my whole being.

You have had the experience of listening to music and feeling your body respond as it begins to move in rhythm with the music?

DAVID: Yes.

MARIEL: Then you know there is no thought involved in this. The music touches your body's own rhythm, and you begin to move accordingly, without thinking about it. When I feel the *anwa* of another, I share their movement. I automatically move in rhythm with it as my own *anwa* responds. It's why I speak of *anwa* in terms of dance and music. And it's why I referred to us as Dancers in the card deck which I gave you. *Anwa* is a being's dance.

The challenge I find with grasping the nature of *anwa* is that it is so close to concepts and experiences with which I'm familiar, such as feeling the energy field around someone or something, that it's easy to think of *anwa* as something it's not. Mariel is explicit that *anwa* is not an energy field in the way I think of energy fields. Yet *anwa* surrounds and imbues its source whether it's a person, a thing, or a place. In this sense, I do find Mariel's reference to dancing helpful. I can picture a person having their own way of moving their body, their own way of engaging with the music and with a partner. It's not a "field" around them; it's the natural rhythm and movement of their bodies, but it only emerges when that person is dancing, whether with another or by themselves in response to music. *Anwa* speaks of potential as well, as much as of what is being actualized in the moment.

In the following conversation, Mariel describes how she came to know her own *anwa*.

MARIEL: When we are children—and yes, I was once a child, though it was a very long time ago as you perceive time—one of the things we must learn is how to distinguish our *anwa* from that of our surroundings. Think of it as coming into a choir and on your first day, needing to hear your part distinct from the parts that everyone else is singing. At first, what you hear may overwhelm you, and you begin singing other people's parts. You need to listen to yourself and be aware of your part, your song. For you in your world and with your bodies, this comes automatically, but for us, we must put intention into this and learn it. We all have individuality, but we are not as aware of it when we are children. We are lost in the songs of the world.

I will tell you a story of my own childhood. When it was time for me to know myself and my *anwa*, my family took me to what in your world would be a cave. I am not sure how to describe this to you, as it was not a physical cavern such as you would have, but it was a place attuned to the interiority of the earth. We went deep into this place where we could find the silence we needed. Not all do this, you understand. Places of silence can be anywhere, but for us, it was in the earth. My family suspected what my *anwa* was and knew that I could best hear it embraced by the energy and spirit of the earth.

I was surrounded with an aura of love and peace, an aura of silence. Everyone sat around me as I was instructed to go within and listen to the song of my being. Because we were away from the world and in this place of silence, this was easy to do as I was not distracted. I listened. I heard many things which I recognized as part of my song, my personal *anwa*. Then I heard something very faint and sweet. I had to reach for it and pay close attention to it. In this, I was helped by the presence of the earth energies around me which acted to amplify this presence and to support me as I attuned to it. As I listened, I was no longer within the earth. I was surrounded by stars. I felt their song, their motion, their *anwa*, and I felt a resonance in myself. A part of me was singing a star song with them.

This part of my *anwa* was hard for me to hold as a child, but the earth around me in the cave held it with me. Isn't this a paradox? Deep in the earth, I could hear the stars, partly because of the silence, but mostly because the strength of the earth gave me the strength to hold this song in myself.

In this way, I began to hear my own *anwa* and began to differentiate myself from the world around me more fully than I had done up to then. I began to become my own being. Part of who I am is connected to the stars. I am a connecting point for their energies and qualities. It is why, when you sensed this because of your own familiarity with those energies, I seemed to be what you called a "star priestess." What you are sensing, though, in your images of me working in my "temple" is my *anwa*. It shows you both who I am and what I do—the motion of my being outward into the world.

When I'm in touch with Mariel, I feel as if the ability to sense and work with *anwa* is much of what makes a Sidhe a Sidhe. If this is true, then it's easy to understand the importance of this concept to a Sidhe. It seems innate to their nature, at least from her perspective and experience. But this creates the second challenge. Does one need to be a Sidhe to sense *anwa*? After all, our worlds are very different, and we are differently constituted. The Sidhe are sensitive to their surroundings in ways we generally are not. What is *anwa* to a human? How might we work with this concept? Can we even be aware of it? I put this question to Mariel.

DAVID: So, you have advice on how we may open to *anwa*?

MARIEL: I said that we experience ourselves as singers in a choir, blending our song with those of others and with a music that is greater than all of us. You, on the other hand, feel yourself to be a solo singer with the music coming from within you. You automatically sing your own melody. What you need to learn is that you are also part of a choir. You need to listen to the melodies of others so you can blend with them, and you all need to hear that music that is larger than your individual parts. That, I think, is the way to discovering the *anwa* in your world.

For example, if you sing in a choir, you sing a part which is arranged to fit harmoniously with other parts. This part is important. You must sing it clearly and strongly, for it is part of your *anwa*, part of who you are. But if you sing this part all by yourself, it may sound strange, for it is designed to blend with other parts in harmony. It is incomplete on its own. If you pay attention to this, you will begin to listen to the other songs and learn how they can blend harmoniously with yours. That blending is also part of *anwa*. It is, as you would say, the felt sense of how you harmonize with what is around you.

I am saying that there is an incompleteness to an individual when he or she considers themselves only as an individual. The feeling of your individuality is not your *anwa*, though it is part of it. When you begin to see how you fit with others, then you begin to sense the rest of your *anwa*. Do you understand? Your *anwa* is not the same as your unique soul. It is, as you would say, how the intent of your soul comes uniquely into being through its relationship—its singing—with the rest of the world. It is the movement of your soul in the world set into motion by your identity but not fully defined by it.

Thinking about this and trying to attune to my own *anwa*, I come back to this idea of "coming into being." This is the idea that there is an "I"—an identity—that is unfolding, but it's not unfolding in a unilateral and unconditioned manner. It is shaped by the way it connects to the world and thus by what the world draws forth. Metaphorically, it unfolds through dance. How I dance is determined by the nature of the music to which I'm dancing but it also depends on the structure and nature of my body, as well as on the relationship I have with my dancing partner. All this dynamic is contained, it seems to me, in the concept of *anwa*.

When Mariel speaks of *anwa*, I am sometimes reminded of the familiar phrase, "to walk in another's shoes." If I understand Mariel, then *anwa* is both the shape and structure of a pair of shoes as well as how a person walks in them. This walk, to continue the metaphor, is different if I am wearing sneakers or high heels, and it's also different if I'm walking on a smooth floor or a gravel path. So, attuning to another's *anwa* is like stepping into their shoes and walking around on their ground, and attuning to the *anwa* of the world is like stepping into the world's shoes—or, in the phrase I use, learning to "think like a planet."

What is very clear is that Mariel is pointing to the importance of our learning to attune to the life in the world around us, including in those things we think of as "non-living." She attunes in this way through *anwa*, and it comes naturally to her to do so. Perhaps we can as well, or perhaps we have a different way of doing so. In any event, she wants the "choir" of the world to succeed, and for this to happen, we not only need to sing our parts but do so in harmony with all the other voices. Indeed, she said as much in one comment that she made during one of our conversations.

> **MARIEL:** You struggle to understand because you want to know what *anwa* is. Think instead of what it does. *Anwa* is important to us because it defines how we engage with something in our world. When we sense the *anwa* around a person or a thing, we can see how to come into harmony with them, how we may best dance with them. It tells us how their being is moving into the world and externalizing itself, and this allows us to blend with that externalization.
>
> The question you should be asking is not, can you sense *anwa*? The question is, can you sense another in a way that allows you to blend with them and draw out their possibilities in harmony with your own? Can you sense another in a way that honors who they are and assists them in being who they are? Can you sense another in a way that enables you to form deep connections?

From Mariel's point of view, in the dance of our being, we humans are constantly bumping into and stepping on the toes of the other dancers in our world. If we could only see or be attuned to how others move, we could avoid this. We could come into a mutually complementing dance. This, to her, is what knowledge of *anwa* would allow us to do.

From my point of view, it is what love and mindfulness allow us to do.

I realize that I may not need to know my *anwa* or that of another as long as I can be openhearted, sensitive to the other, caring, loving, listening, observing—in short, acting in whatever way will optimize harmony between us and be mutually empowering. I can use *anwa* as a concept inspiring me to find my human equivalent as the way I can create harmony. It may be very useful and wonderful to sense the actual *anwa* itself, but as Mariel suggested, it might not be as easy for a human being as it is for a Sidhe.

Then again, maybe all it takes is practice.

I spent some time trying to tune in to my *anwa* and that of things around me. Sometimes, I felt I had it; at other times, it was elusive, like the feeling you have when something is just on the tip of your tongue but you can't quite capture it. When next we had a conversation, she commented on this.

> **MARIEL:** I have been observing you, and if you allow me to say so, you are going about it in a wrong fashion. I understand that you need to think into these things, and that thinking is part of your mode of attunement. It is part of your *anwa*. But from my point of view, you cannot attune to *anwa* the way you might attune to an organ in your body or to your subtle energy field. Instead, you must surrender to its motion and allow it to carry you into itself.

> **DAVID:** I'm sure you're sensing I have a question about this!

> **MARIEL:** Yes, so pay attention! *Anwa* is not something you have but something you do, and this doing arises from who you are. *Anwa* is the song of your whole self singing in joy for being alive and in the world. I realize that what I have not said clearly is that joy is the essence of *anwa*. You have a phrase, "doing your happy dance." *Anwa* is your happy dance, your happy song. Be with yourself in joy—be joyous in being yourself and in being in your world—and you will feel your *anwa*.

> Let me use an example. Let us say I wish to attune to the *anwa*

of a tree. Yes, we can use your maple tree in your backyard as the example. The *anwa* would not exist if the structure and form of the tree did not exist. Its roots, its trunk, its bark, its branches, its leaves, all these are part of its *anwa*. But they are not the whole of it. Nor is the subtle energy aura of the tree the *anwa*. I want to be aware of these things, but to feel the *anwa*, I must look between and beyond them. You have a phrase, "to read between the lines;" *anwa* exists between the lines, so to speak.

What is between the lines of your maple tree? Here I find the joy that holds the whole together. This is a joy of being—of having structure, of having bark and trunk, roots and branches and all the rest of it. It is also a joy of connection to its world, to the soil, to the birds, to the small animals that run along its limbs, and yes, to you as a human friend who takes delight in its presence. This joy is a substance to me. It is the medium in which the *anwa* exists, just as air is a medium in which the sound of a song exists. And for each being, this joy is shaped in a way that depends on its nature, just as the sound of each song is its own thing.

DAVID: So let me go back to something you said some years ago about shapeshifting. You spoke then of taking on the *anwa* of the form into which you were changing your shape. You said knowing the *anwa* was necessary to this process. What you're implying here is that you take on that creature's joy in being itself, in having the shape it has and in the way that shape lets it engage the world.

MARIEL: Yes. We enter the joy of another. Let me ask you a question. How now do you think you can discover your *anwa*?

DAVID: By acknowledging and stepping into the joy I feel at being who and what I am both as a unique person and as a part of this world.

MARIEL: Yes. It's simple when you put it this way. *Anwa* is not just joy alone as a quality, but it is joy that gives your song of life its body and resonance. It is joy as a vibration of being.

And why might this be relevant to you as a human?

DAVID: I see what you're getting at. One way I can attune to my world is to attune to its joy of being. For instance, the *anwa* of my wife, Julie, is the pattern created by her joy at being who she is, and if I can share and participate in that joy, I attune to her *anwa*.

MARIEL: This is the place to start. There is more than just this to *anwa*, but this is how to begin. Discover and stand in your joy of being. Let that joy carry you into the song of your life, the dance of your life, the *anwa* of your life. Remember, I said that *anwa* was the motion of your spirit as it engages life, and joy is the essence of this motion. It defines this motion.

As you gain sensitivity to this motion in you by opening your awareness to the joy of your life, then you will learn how to attune to the *anwa* of others. Remember, this isn't simply an act of mind; it is a resonance of the heart. It is you sharing with them their joy at being. Don't think about it. Allow this joy to flow into you and meet your own. This cannot help but open deeper and more harmonious connections between you.

In the larger picture, we wish to help you come into greater harmony with your world. We believe, my colleagues and I, that if you learn to live into the *anwa* of the world, the joy within the world, this deeper harmony will develop.

I am complete for now. Blessings to you and to all who read the words you will write from our exchange.

One morning as I was nearing completion on this book, Mariel came to me and said she had something to say about *anwa* and imagination. I wasn't sure just where to put this conversation, since it could easily go into the previous chapter on imagination or it could go here as part of the discussion of *anwa*. I decided on the latter since the discussion went beyond just the imagination to add more to our understanding of *anwa*.

MARIEL: For us, *anwa* is part of the life of everything we see and touch. It is therefore part of how we imagine as well. For the most part, your imagination focuses upon form. Our imagination, on the other hand, is one of life. Your very word *imagination* conveys the way you think about this. You form a picture in your mind and call that imagining. When we imagine something, we think of its *anwa* as well as its form. Indeed, as our sense of the *anwa* grows in us, the form that matches it may emerge. However, this happens in us, we are experiencing a living presence and not just forming a picture.

DAVID: There is an exercise in visualization training in which you are asked to imagine a fruit like an orange. Rather than just have a mental picture by itself, you go further to imagine its qualities and attributes, such as what it feels like, what it smells like, the taste of it in your mouth, its texture, and so forth. All of this is to build a complete sensory experience of the orange in your imagination. So, we also can go beyond simple pictures in how we use our imaginations.

MARIEL: Yes, this is true, and I did not mean to limit your imaginative capacities. But in your example, you are still imagining the physical form of the orange, yes? All that you have mentioned are qualities perceivable by your physical senses. To grasp the *anwa* of the orange is to know its life in the world, the motion of its spirit outward into the world to connect and to know itself as the world knows it. This knowledge is beyond the senses.

I am not sure just how to describe this to you. It is like describing a color to someone who has never seen it but could see it if alerted to its presence. Think of it this way. To us, there is an intelligence behind the orange; there is a spirit that lies at the root of it and is the cause of its coming into being. This intelligence wishes to communicate something to the world, and the orange is how it does so. But this communication is not one-way. This intelligence listens to the world as well and finds how it can add to the conversation of life around it. So, when it speaks and the orange comes into being, the life and form of the orange contain both what this intelligence wished to say shaped by what the world wished to hear and how this statement of "orange" fits into the planetary conversation. This communication is the *anwa*. It is what a being says about who it is, but it is also what the world says about who it is and how it fits, as nothing exists in isolation. Everything is part of the conversation of life. And as I have said, there is joy in this conversation.

DAVID: *Anwa* is a part of manifestation, then. Yes, I understand this. It is like the concepts I employ in how I teach manifestation. Manifestation always takes place in a system of connectedness and interdependency.

MARIEL: Yes.

DAVID: But here is where I need clarification. We use imagination not just to form an image of something, but we can imagine how it is connected, how it fits into a larger context, as well. In fact, this is an important part of how I teach manifestation. For me, manifestation is not simply an act of attracting something into your life. As you would say, that only operates at the level of form. I see manifestation as an act of incarnation, specifically the incarnation of the person doing the manifestation. Therefore, the process I teach asks a person to imagine how that which she wishes to manifest connects to the whole of her life and her interactions with the world. How does it fit, for in a way, it is this fit, this connection, that she is manifesting, not just the desired object or situation. So, is this "fit" the same as *anwa*? It sounds to me like this is what you're saying here.

MARIEL: It is close, yes. But be careful that you are not simply thinking of the physical fit of something. *Anwa* is not a shape like a puzzle piece that you are fitting into a larger picture. It is not static. But your comments help me to further see this through your eyes, and I think we are closer to communicating together the nature of anwa, at least as we experience it. As I have said, it may be different for you as your world and ours are very different.

DAVID: Then I have another thought. It also seems to me as I think about it that *anwa* is akin to what we might mean by a person's calling or his soul's intent. Is this a fair comparison?

MARIEL: Again, it is close, but if I understand what you are saying, it is not identical. A calling may be part of a person's *anwa* but it does not define it. You would need to also see how that calling engages with the world. What is a natural way, inherent in both the individual and in the world, for that calling to be expressed and fulfilled. Remember, *anwa* is dynamic. It is a motion outward into the world and how that motion is shaped by the world. *Anwa* is the pattern created as the soul flows into your life and as your life flows into your world.

DAVID: Can a person's *anwa* change, then, as the world changes or as the person changes? Do I have one *anwa* when I am born but a different one perhaps when I grow older?

MARIEL: *Anwa* can change but normally it is stable throughout a person's life. How a being's *anwa* manifests can change, but the *anwa* itself changes little. For example, your *anwa* reflects how you fit into and engage the human race of which you are a part. It is not fundamentally changed by whether you are living in one society or another, whether you are in America or in China. How you express your *anwa* will differ depending on the society in which you are living, but your *anwa* will remain constant.

I believe I should leave it at this and allow this concept to grow in you like a seed. I fear too many words will lead you to over think this matter, and at heart, it is not a matter of thought. *Anwa* is something we feel and perceive, as much a part of anything we see as its form or its texture. It is an expression of its life in harmony with the life of the world. There is not much more I can say about it except to repeat that if you use your imagination to grasp the nature of *anwa*, imagine life and not just form, even if that form is subtle and energetic in nature. *Anwa* is not another term for the subtle body, but it is a description of the life that flows from all parts of you, the joyous motion of your spirit in all the levels of the world you inhabit.

Blessings!

Mariel originally introduced the concept of *anwa* to me when she was describing the creation of a building. She said that at the beginning of the process, the builders would tune into the *anwa* of the building. In this context, the word seemed to mean both the purpose and identity of the building and also how it fit into the environment. *Anwa*, as I understood it at the time, seemed to exist at the interface of being and doing and had a strong relational quality to it.

The Sidhe seem to live in a world of *anwa*. Everything possesses it; being sensitive to it, it affects how they relate to each other and to the things around them, being respectful of the life and purpose of what is unfolding in each other and in the things and creatures of the world. They want to serve how something fits in. Fitting in is a matter of connection and coherency, so *anwa* has to do with understanding and fostering coherency.

For Mariel, *anwa* is a dynamic concept. Take the example of a chair. Its *anwa* is its identity as a chair as well as how it fits into the world. But this "fitting in" is flexible. A chair might at times be used as a footstool or a table, or even as something to stand on. In all these cases, the *anwa* of the chair is about providing support, whatever form that support takes. This is how a chair fits into its world.

Anwa for the Sidhe is a practical, not a philosophical, matter. It enables them to see, to honor, and to assist both the identity and the "fitting in" of something or someone they encounter. It helps them fit in to the nature of that which they are encountering, all in service to promoting coherency and wholeness in the world.

MARIEL'S WORLD

Over the years of our association, I've had several impressions of Mariel's world. These are side effects of our "being-meld," images that have been left in my mind after the contact has ended. Rather than forming a coherent whole, however, these images were often contradictory or confusing at best. For instance, several times I had an image of a city near to where she lives most of the time, but these images varied. At times, it was an urban metropolis, at other times, more like a large village. Likewise, I had mental pictures of Mariel living in a village-like community and then I would have impressions of her living alone like a hermit high on the slopes of a mountain. Sometimes she seemed aloof and solitary, at other times communal and gregarious, blending into the company of other Sidhe. Even Mariel herself seemed different at different times. She always carries herself with power and authority, but sometimes it is more evident and she fairly glows with her presence, but at other times she seems muted to me, almost as if she were a different person.

I put these contradictions down to the inability of my mind to fully grasp the complexity and strangeness of the Sidhe world. I knew how my imagination would attempt to resolve confusing impressions into familiar images. So, I did the best I could to accurately represent what I was receiving from her mind and being and left the rest to sort itself out over time. In preparing for this book, however, I felt I wanted greater clarity about Mariel's world, so over several contacts, I asked her a series of questions. In doing so, though, I sometimes sensed a reluctance on her part to go into much detail.

DAVID: Mariel, I would appreciate your clarification of the images I hold about you and your world. Like many, I am curious and wish to understand you and your environment more fully.

MARIEL: I appreciate that you have questions. I honor the fact that you wish to know more about me and about my world. When possible, I shall try to answer you. But I am reluctant to give too much detail. The reason for this is the same as why we asked you not to portray us in illustrations for the cards. We do not wish to predetermine how someone will experience us; we do not wish to create too many thought-forms and images about us lest they constrict our connections rather than expand them. We would rather each person discover in his or her own way who we are in relationship to who they are. We wish to be welcoming to all comers whatever their background and tradition.

Our worlds are different. This makes it hard for me to describe my world as it is; I must translate its nature into images that are meaningful to you, and even then, if may be hard for you to fully conceive of it; therefore, anything you write carries the potential to be misconstrued and perhaps taken too literally.

For instance, you are more differentiated beings than we are. Our inner nature is not so divided into mental and emotional aspects. I cannot tell you how we think or how we feel because we do so in very different ways from you. As I have said at other times, you are worlds unto yourselves, which is both a strength and a challenge for you. We are not so enclosed. We have individuality, but at the same time we are a more flowing part of the world, and we think and feel in concert with the world.

Words like *individual* and *collective* are not adequate to describe our nature. Where we are concerned, they distort as much as inform. Perhaps a way to say this is that we have *participatory individuality*, and *anwa* is a key to that participation.

I would tell you, though, that from our perspective, you are not that divided, either. You fill yourselves with thoughts and self-images that create boundaries, both within yourselves and within your world. I understand why this is so, but it does not define your essential nature. You are all more whole beings than you give yourselves credit for being. You are also participatory individuals. This, I think, is what you are starting to remember.

Now, let me use a metaphor. You live horizontally as if on a flat world whereas we live horizontally and vertically as if in a spherical world. I have already said that you are like land creatures while we are like creatures of the ocean. You move horizontally across the landscape, but we move up and down within the sea as well.

This means that our world has landscapes much like your own, but these landscapes exist on multiple levels of perception and energy. Some are very close to your world and here and there merge with the physical dimension; in such cases, the land mimics your land closely, and the two may affect each other. Other landscapes in our world are far removed from your dimension; they are in the upper levels of the sphere, so to speak. These landscapes are not affected by nor do they affect your world, and those who live there are often far removed from human affairs through their own choice.

My home of origin, so to speak, is in the upper reaches of our world, though not at the highest levels. But I am now living in what you might think of as a "forward base," one that is established on a level closer to your world to make contact easier. You might say that here I am in the middle of the sphere. I live in a community of like-minded colleagues, and together we form an association that is dedicated to establishing and developing lines of contact and collaboration with you. Our community—what you might think of as our village—is new as these things go in my world.

The landscape in which I live is not close enough to you to mimic your landscape, but there are correspondences. You have many mountains in your physical landscape; I have one, but my one mountain has roots in your world and extends vibrationally into the upper reaches of my own. In this manner, this mountain is tied to your mountains through these roots. I draw upon the energy of the mountain spirit to make connections with your world because it straddles both.

Your people settle in areas because the land offers resources. We do the same. The resources that are meaningful to us, however, are vibrational; they are resources of energy and connection. The presence of this mountain and its overlighting spirit is just such a resource, especially for the work we wish to do with you. Likewise, the rich natural energies of the forests and water in your physical landscape provide resonances and currents that we can use as well. Though this is not my native landscape, I have moved here for the benefits this landscape provides, just as you have done on your level of life in the physical world.

DAVID: You say this is not your native land. Are you from another part of the world? Do you come, for instance, from the Celtic lands such as Ireland?

MARIEL: Ah, you see, this is what I meant about the challenge of conveying the nature of our world to you. You are thinking of a single layer of land and sea that covers the globe. Our world is not constructed in this way. I used the image of the sphere to suggest that we live on multiple layers of life and energy and can rise and lower ourselves between them, much as a fish can go up and down in the ocean. But our world is not a globe in the way yours is. There are landscapes that are tied to your physical dimension, places where our world and yours touch, but much of our world has no direct correspondence to your own.

What I think of as my "native land" is at another vibrational level, as I have said. I cannot describe it to you for it does not have what you would think of as a solid physical appearance. It is shaped by our personal and collective imaginations and desires, and thus its appearance is fluid. This may sound chaotic to you, but I assure you, it is not. There is order based on principles of interconnection not dissimilar to those you find in your study of ecology. Further, we have landmarks and features in the landscape—the equivalent to what you have as mountains and forests, plains and rivers, but they do not look the same. They are a part of us as well as being outside of us, or I might say, we are a part of them. They are living fields of energy and consciousness which if translated into your world would become what you know as forests and mountains and other features of your landscape. You might say we live in the midst of the life and spirit of trees or rivers, mountains or plains; we live in connection with their *anwa*. But this life and spirit can take any form. If I wish to have fir trees around me, then fir trees will manifest, not out of nothing but out of the *anwa* of the living field of trees that form part of my landscape. Or I may simply enjoy the presence of Tree in all its richness without the need for it to take a specific form.

When I said that where I live now is not my land of origin, I meant only that I originated on a level of our world more distant from the physical. It would not have any correspondence directly with any part of your physical world but is very much in touch with the spirit of Gaia. Where I live now is closer to your plane, though still removed enough that I can do my inner work as what you call a "priestess." We draw on the energies of the mountain and the forests to be here, and from this place, we can move into closer proximity with where you are. For me, these moments of contact are necessarily short, but there are others of our association who are native to this level or even lower, in the sense of being closer to the physical, and thus can stay in contact with you for longer periods of time.

The land where I live now would be more familiar to you as it is less fluid and malleable than in the realms where I originated. As you have seen in your inner sight, here the mountain is a mountain and the forests are forests, much as they are in your world. But even here, your imagination fails to see all that is there so that what you see as my mountain or my forest is pale and static compared to what I perceive and experience.

Remember, I am not always as you see me. The Mariel who speaks to you now is a form partly woven out of my attunement to your land and your imagination, as you know. What you see is not quite the same as the Mariel who lives amongst her people in her community. When I am doing my inner work, contacting the stellar energies or communing with those from my native level or higher, then I am a different Mariel yet again

DAVID: You would appear as a swirling mist of Light as when I first saw you?

MARIEL (laughing): Maybe. I don't know. What you saw then was not my higher form but simply my energy adjusting and configuring to your own to take on a shape appropriate to your mind and your world. But what you would see of my higher form, I cannot say. It is possible you would not see me at all. What I look like is influenced by the qualities I take on coming from the sources with which I am in contact. It's the same process in principle as when I contact you.

DAVID: But I suppose there is a "real" Mariel in there somewhere, a Mariel that you are most of the time?

MARIEL: All of me is the real Mariel, just as all of you is the real David. The Mariel you see now is not a "made-up" Mariel, simply one shaped to better engage with you. But yes, I have a constant form and appearance suitable to the community and landscape I inhabit most of the time. Just remember that we are shape-shifters!

DAVID: Mariel, you often mention your city. Is it like a city in my world?

MARIEL: Many of the reasons you have for building cities are superfluous or unimportant to us. We do not engage in commerce as you do, hence we have no need for market places. We do not need places of government, nor do we have industry in the same way you do. The driving force for us in coming together and creating a city is to enhance our creativity and life energy through proximity and sharing. A city for us is a way of blending our energies to draw more deeply and richly on the energies of Gaia, something we can do when gathered together more fully than when we are alone.

I can see in your mind that you might imagine a Sidhe city as a colorful, gleaming place with soaring towers. Certainly, such a place is possible if the inhabitants would wish to create it so. Our cities might be best understood as collective art works. So, they vary in appearance. Some can be quite ornate, at least for as long as its inhabitants desire it. Others are much simpler. They provide places of residence, places of gathering and community, places of creative work.

I said there is no commerce. From your point of view, this is true. We do not buy or sell as you do. But we do create objects of art or utility, and there is an exchange of energy that takes place between the creator and the "purchaser." If I make an object, I do so not to sell it but as an expression of my creative relationship with my world; it is an expression of my craftsmanship. If I wish to share my creations, I can give them away, or I may indeed have a "store" in which I display them so that others may enjoy and appreciate them and, if they wish, take them into their own lives. They do not purchase them with money as you would do, but there would be an exchange of living energy between us that I would find enhancing. You might see it as a gift of love and appreciation on their part, but it is more than an emotion. My energy field is empowered by their gift, just as my creation enhances theirs. When we can have a direct exchange of energy in this way, we have no need for its symbolic representation in the form of coinage.

A city provides a convenient place for these kinds of exchanges to take place, so in that sense, you could say there is a market. But mainly, it is a place where we can accomplish those things that cannot be done alone but which are only possible—or are better done—when a group is present.

My city is on the slopes of a mountain to take advantage of the range of energies and connections the mountain and its spirit provide. As I described, this mountain is not a direct replica of your nearby mountain [*which would be Mt. Rainier—David*]. You might say it is a composite in our realm of the mountains that exist around you in yours. It draws on and stores the energy of all these mountains. My city is where it is precisely so it can draw on these energies, thereby connecting us in a powerful way to the planetary life of Gaia.

If you were to visit my city, I'm not sure what you would see. The city exists on several levels of energy and by its nature—and its proximity to the mountain—makes shifting between these levels easier than when done alone. What you would see would depend on the range of your vision and the levels of "city-ness" to which you could attune. I am aware of all of them, but you may not be. Indeed, your thought-form of soaring spires and towers as part of a Sidhe city is a way your mind might attempt to understand and interpret the energetic impression you have of those elements of our city that extend into the higher levels of energy. If you saw it at the level closest to your world, it would likely seem small and simple to you, more like a village or a hamlet. It is in the higher frequencies of its nature that the city grows in size, complexity, and beauty.

Let me share with you a recent visit I made to the city which may illustrate its nature. This visit was brought about by a visit by a Sidhe elder who was one of my teachers in the past and remains a friend. On this occasion, he was giving a talk in the city. As he is eloquent and insightful, this alone would have been reason to go. But I also needed his advice concerning my own work. Had this been an urgent matter, I could have visited him where he lives in the upper ranges of our world. But as he was coming into the city, it was an opportunity to consult with him on the level where I spend most of my time.

On this level, our city is a simple one. It is smaller and perhaps more what you might think of as a town. However, I can always access the city on its higher levels. When I do, it becomes larger and more populated for on those levels it is less remote and more accessible.

In this case, my teacher was giving a talk in a hall that exists on a higher level. Which gave him access to a broader range of energies to use in his presentation. It also facilitated the blessings of energy that he wished to offer to those attending. Had I wished, I could have attended his talk on a lower level of the city, but in so doing, I would have missed much of what he was offering.

Going to the "upper city" is simply a matter of adjusting my consciousness and drawing upon the living mind and spirit of the city itself to make the shift. You often have this image of our cities gleaming with Light and color and possessing tall spires reaching into the heavens. In this instance, you would not have been disappointed, for in resonance with his presentation and the energies he was invoking and generating, the hall we were in did indeed develop a spire of energy that rose into the heavens. When he was complete, we visited for a time, and then I returned to my community in its place closer to your world. As I did so, the city changed its shape and complexity accordingly.

I hope this satisfies some of your curiosity!

Jeremy Berg, my partner in co-creating the *Card Deck of the Sidhe*, will sometimes travel to give workshops and lectures on the Sidhe. On a couple of occasions, he was contacted by Sidhe individuals native to the place where he happened to be who mentioned being contacted by Mariel who had asked them to help Jeremy. This got me wondering about the extent of her connections.

DAVID: Mariel, are you connected with Sidhe in other parts of the world?

MARIEL (laughing): Are you not connected to humans in other parts of the world? Your electronic devices allow you to communicate anywhere in the world. We can do the same, though through entirely different means. Why should we be isolated? When there is need, we can reach out and make contact with others of our kind.

Many Sidhe are connected to and shaped by the land in which we live and even, if they live close to your dimension, by the landscape of the physical earth. In this regard, you might say we are territorial. While there are those amongst us who love to travel, most of us remain in one place and are defined by the characteristics of that place. However, we are not limited to just where our bodies may be. We can participate in a web of energy, Light, and consciousness that links us together when we wish to do so. Also, because we are more engaged with the life of Gaia, it would be appropriate to say that we occupy the world in its wholeness, not only the places where our bodies are located.

Thus, if our bodies do not travel much, our minds can. You do the same. Through your technology, you can be present most places in your world, and you can speak with people far distant from you. This is true for us, as well.

Along a similar line of questioning, I have friends in different parts of the world who have felt themselves in touch with the Sidhe. Four of them have written books about their experiences: John Matthews in Britain whose contact led him to write *The Sidhe* and most recently, to create a new card deck, *The Moon Oracle of the Sidhe*; Anne Gambling in Switzerland, who wrote *Awakening to Home* of her many experiences of Sidhe contact; Søren Hauge from Denmark whose contact with a Nordic Sidhe named Fjeldur led to him writing *The Wild Alliance*; and Geoffrey Oelsner in the United States who describes his experiences in *A Country*

Where All Colors Are Alive. These are all excellent books. They illustrate the wide distribution and variety of Sidhe contact. At the same time, they bring up a question I am frequently asked: "Are the Sidhe the same everywhere?" I asked this of Mariel.

> **MARIEL**: Are humans the same everywhere? You are one species but with wide variations and differences. The same is true for us, with two additional elements. The first is that the fluidity and plasticity of our forms gives rise to even more variation than is possible for you in your physical state. You should not forget that we can be shape-changers. The second is that, as I have said, our world possesses several layers of energy and consciousness. Depending on the level a Sidhe occupies, he or she will have differing characteristics.
>
> You should not put us all the same category. Sidhe come in many sizes and flavors, as you would say. We have varied interests and concerns, just as you do. We are not as large a population as humanity. We are nevertheless a global species the same as you, though, as I have been saying, we occupy the world differently from you.

As she described this, I had an interesting image. Our physical earth has geographical zones from the frigid climate of the Artic to the hot Tropical Zone along the Equator. Humans inhabit all of them, but the human types and cultures that have evolved in these zones are different from each other, especially between the extremes. There is no confusing the life of an Amazonian Indian with that of an Alaskan Eskimo.

> **MARIEL**: There is a third element. As I have said, we are very long-lived if we choose to be. We do not have the same need to reproduce as often as you. For this reason, we do not have as many children as you do, and those we have tend to come in cycles in a rhythm tied to the needs of Gaia and the Sidhe rather than to the needs of individuals.
>
> Thus, we can be differentiated by the generation to which we belong, as each generation can have its distinguishing vibration and qualities. There are Sidhe who are very ancient even by our standards. Some of these individuals have forsaken the physical

earth and humanity and live in distant levels in our world. Some of the older generations act as Elders, providing guidance and insight. Some have been involved for hundreds of your years with certain places in your world, a relationship that in some cases developed before humans were present. These Sidhe continue to act as guardians of the life and well-being of such places, working closely with the spirits of nature. Should you encounter of one these guardians, he or she may not seem like a Sidhe at all but more like a spirit of nature.

Though I am several hundred of your years in age, I am part of a newer generation. There are two younger generations after mine, and these younger Sidhe are in many instances closer to you and the human world. They are forerunners of a time when our two peoples and our two worlds will work and blend in greater collaboration.

Jeremy Berg has told me that when he travels, there are places where he feels the Sidhe to be more accessible than in other places. I asked Mariel about this.

MARIEL: It is true. Our world touches yours more closely in some places than in others. The presence of strong nature energies in the landscape draws our world closer to you. In places where human presence and activity are strong, we are less accessible as a rule. Bu there are exceptions. Though I am not one of them, there are some Sidhe who are drawn to your cities, mainly out of curiosity but sometimes to be of service.

As I said, our population is smaller than yours, and there is much of your land that is not in direct contact with us or with our world, though it may be in touch with our intermediaries. There are places in your world where the living energies of Gaia are strongly concentrated. These are often areas you would deem wilderness, but this is not always the case. The energetic legacy of past human and Sidhe collaboration can build fields of resonance and memory that are still extant, though perhaps dormant. As a general rule, whether through intention or a consequence of natural forces and landscape, where Gaian energies are concentrated is where we will settle and be found in greater numbers. After all, when you build your cities, it is usually near water or some other important natural resource. The living energies of Gaia or of the cosmos beyond are our vital resources; where they are strong, there we will likely be as well.

Throughout these conversations, there was an image that kept tickling at the back of my mind, something that was part of the meaning of what Mariel was trying to tell me but which I simply wasn't grasping. This isn't unusual, whether I'm in touch with Mariel or with any of the subtle colleagues I normally work with. We can have conversations that would appear normal in our world, but much of the time, the information or message comes as what I experience as a "spherical download." That is, all the information and all the interconnections between bits of information (like hypertext connections in an electronic digital document) comes as a single, complete whole, rather than being strung out linearly the way we talk, one word and one concept following another. It's like suddenly knowing everything at once about the topic at hand, which can be overwhelming. I then must sort through this download and turn it into a sequence of ideas to present it verbally. Sometimes in this process, something gets overlooked or lost, or I'm not sure at first where it fits, so I set the impulse or impression aside.

In this case, it had to do with Sidhe "land" and its proximity and resonance with physical landscapes. Finally, one morning when working on something else entirely, the penny dropped, as they say, and what Mariel had said came more fully into focus. Later, I had an opportunity to ask her questions.

MARIEL: You could say that in the ecology of our world, there are three kinds of landscapes. There is our world proper which reflects our nature. It is this world that is hard for me to describe to you. Then there are landscapes that are close to your own and that mimic to a greater or lesser degree what is present in the physical world. So, if you have a lake, we would have a lake as well; if you have a mountain, we would have a mountain. But these places are not that common. More common is a third condition in which we occupy a landscape that is invented, so to speak, and constructed to have resonance with your world but still be part of our world. These "lands" are not fully in your world or ours but occupy a middle ground that is accessible to both. I occupy such a land much of the time in my work with you.

The advantage of such an intermediate land is that it assists us in connecting with the vibrations and conditions of your world, which for many of us are challenging.

DAVID: This is what you meant by a "forward base."

MARIEL: Yes, though I got the image from your mind. It is a base camp, a bridging world familiar enough in appearance and energy to connect both of our dimensions. Such a land can be in touch with several places on the earth simultaneously, and will mold itself to the local terrain in your world to anchor itself. So, I can be in my village and be equally in touch with you where you live or with someone in another part of your world.

DAVID: Is your city part of this forward base camp as well?

MARIEL: In its lower vibratory levels, yes. But the main part of the city is wholly in our world and beyond the bridging dimension.

I would caution you not to be too linear in your conception of how our world relates to yours. It's not as if you are climbing a ladder from a bottom rung where the physical world influence is greatest to a top rung where the Sidhe world influence is wholly represented. There are places in your world, places of great natural energy and power where the higher reaches of our world can directly touch your physical plane. And there are places in your world where even the bridging dimension—our forward base camps—have difficulty making a foothold. It is not all dependent on the presence and influence of human energy either. There are places in your natural world where it is difficult for us to go because the energies of nature are too strong for us. Remember, we are not nature spirits, even though we may be confused as being such. You can over romanticize our connection with the natural world, but just as you cannot go into a volcano, there are places where the energies of the earth are too strong for us to bear, no matter how attuned we may be to the natural flow of life. Likewise, there are places in your cities where human energies are densest that are nonetheless very close to and even touching our realm. Think of swimming in cold water and suddenly encountering a warm patch that is comfortable and sustaining to you.

I say this so that you don't form mental images of our world that are rigid or that conform to some vertical spectrum of energy progression. There can be truth to such a spectrum, but it is not the whole picture.

These conversations about her world brought up another question for me. Mariel has said repeatedly that the Sidhe are not nature spirits but are a species of humanity (or we may be a species of Sidhe!). Yet in folklore throughout the world, the Sidhe or Sidhe-like beings are included in stories of the Little Folk or the Fey Folk and are often thought of as nature beings. I know the relationship of the Sidhe to these "children of Gaia" can be close and deeply intertwined, just as can be true for some humans. But I nevertheless sought further clarification from Mariel.

DAVID: You said that we may be in touch with you through "intermediaries." Could you elaborate on what you mean by this, please?

MARIEL: The Sidhe have nowhere near your numbers in population, but we extend our energy into your world through collaboration with allies. Many of the elementals and spirits of nature are close to us and can embody our energy even as we can embody theirs. This can make them "Sidhe-like" in your eyes. There is a vast Faerie realm that is kin to us and we to it. They can be mistaken for us and we for them. In many cases, it may not matter, for we can speak with one voice. The difference is that the true Faerie realm is a part of Gaia's being, whereas we, like you, are ancient companions of Gaia come from another source.

There are thought-forms that we have created that can act as our representatives as well. It is also possible that our energy and influence can be augmented and extended by the thought-forms of us that you create. There is a risk here, though, as humans can have images of us that are inaccurate and surrounded with glamour, obstructing contact rather than facilitating it.

DAVID: So in a way, there is a cloud of "Sidhe-ness" surrounding the world.

MARIEL: You could say so, yes, though more concentrated in some places than in others, as I have described.

DAVID: How, then, is a person to know if they are in touch with an actual Sidhe or in touch with the Sidhe-Cloud or with one of the intermediaries?

MARIEL: It may not matter. What needs to be shared or transmitted will be. It may be as well that those in the realm of the nature spirits and of the Faerie Realms may have more to offer a specific person than do we. But if contact with us will be fruitful, then it will come about.

As for how you will know, I can only say, pay attention to what you are feeling in yourself and around that which you are contacting. Remember that we are not nature spirits, but we are concerned with issues of wholeness and creativity. Further, our purpose in connecting with you is to enhance your humanity and your ability to be part of the world in wholeness. If the contact takes you away from the world and your place in it, it is likely not one of my kin.

Perhaps the best I can say is that we are part of each other, children of a shared ancestor. We are not human, as you have learned, but we are cousins in ways you are not with the elementals and beings of nature. So, pay attention to the ties and resonances you feel with that which claims to be Sidhe.

DAVID: My friend John-Matthews in his book *The Sidhe* and now in his new card deck, *The Moon Oracle of the Sidhe*, put forth ways of contacting your people, such as the use of a special glyph. The card deck that you inspired Jeremy and me to create does the same. Obviously, you wish us to contact you. If we use tools like these card decks or the glyph, will we contact you specifically?

MARIEL: Not necessarily. It is possible, for I am linked to that for which I am responsible. Remember that our card deck was a group endeavor; I am not alone in helping to bring it into being. So, it has links to more of us than just me. There is also a matter of individual resonance. Someone other than me may be more suitable for contact with a specific person based on energy affinities.

But the glyph and the card decks act like beacons. They create a focal point of energy designed to connect with the collective energy of the Sidhe, what you are calling the "Sidhe cloud," rather than with a specific individuality. Contact with our collective presence can be instructive and energizing by itself, drawing forth your own inner wisdom and attunement. However, if you are in contact with the collective spirit and mind of the Sidhe, an individual Sidhe can respond if he or she desires to do so. Some areas of the world, as I have said, will bring a quicker, stronger response because our world may be closer to your dimension there, or we have a "forward base" in touch with it, but we have ways of connecting with you through spirit that are not affected by place or time.

THE "STAR PRIESTESS"

One question I had for Mariel was to ask why she contacted me in the first place. Why did she wish to connect with human beings and thus design a card deck for that purpose? She has said that she is the head of an "association" of Sidhe desirous of greater collaboration and who are exploring what this might mean and how to facilitate it. How and why did this association come into being? I asked her this, but her response led—at least initially—into a whole other discussion about the nature of the stellar realms and her work as what I called a "star priestess."

    DAVID: Mariel, why are you working for greater contact and collaboration with human beings?

    MARIEL: The simple answer is that I was asked to do so by the stars. This may seem a strange and glamorous thing to say to you. Behind my statement is a reality that is not at all as simple as it sounds. Nevertheless, the fact is that the stars called me to contact you.

    DAVID: I would like you to explain more fully.

    MARIEL: First you must understand the nature of the stars. I know that you have experience of the living reality that lies behind the lights you see in your night sky. This is one of the factors that creates resonance and connection between us and is a reason I came to you. But you do not understand the stars in the way I do, for it is my *anwa* to be their… emissary. You do not have an appropriate word for what I am.

    DAVID: I have thought of you as a "star-priestess."

    MARIEL: Yes, but this is not accurate, at least this is not what I or my associates would call me. I am a living portal between my world and community and forces from the stellar realms. Because I mediate such forces, you identify me as a priestess, for in your mind, this is what a priest or priestess does. If this is the sum of your meaning, I am happy to be a priestess in your thinking.

However, my work is not religious in nature. We certainly have people who are developed in their spirit and skilled at sharing the gifts such development brings, but this is considered a natural activity, not a special role. No Sidhe requires another to contact or mediate the Sacred for them.

I take substance from the stellar realms, given by the stars, and blend it within myself, in the sanctuary of my being. I bring it into a form that I can pass on to my world.

DAVID: I should call you a "stellar alchemist," then.

MARIEL: If it helps you. You have a greater need for names, I think, than we do. In matters such as this, my *anwa* is my name, the revealer of my identity. And my *anwa* is connected to the stars.

DAVID: I apologize for interrupting. It's important to me to understand what you are and what you do, and I have many questions.

MARIEL: I understand. Your questions are important. I shall come to them, but first I must explain what the stars are to me.

The stellar realms lie close to the mystery of Divinity, and none at our level of consciousness may fully penetrate or know all that they contain or the fullness of their nature. They are beyond all time, space, and matter as we know them. They radiate pure beingness in a manner past our comprehension.

The stellar realms are the mediators through which the life, the joy, the Light of the Sacred enter the cosmos. They are vast and many-layered. There dwell cosmic Intelligences whose physical manifestations take form as stars and clusters of stars, but there are those who do not manifest in such a manner and whose Light you cannot see but who nevertheless hold the universe together. They are the Firstborn of Creation, those Presences who are the first emanations from the Sacred. They are not beings as you would understand that word, but they are not "not-beings," either. They do not fit into any category you have. They are jewels possessing infinite facets of possibility and potential, the matrices from which all manifestation proceeds. Though they are far removed from the plane on which you and I live, yet they are within us as well and within our world, for they are in the substance from which we emerge.

From these Firstborn come those forces and beings who are the immediate origins of the stars as you know them, the progenitors of the physical universe. Here, in realms that are at the edge of accessibility for your consciousness and mine, may be found star-souls and cosmic angels.

As physical stars are the wombs of matter, so the stars of spirit are wombs of life. While I cannot reach into the further reaches of the stellar realms, in those areas to which I can attune I find cosmic beings who midwife the birth and formation of planetary spirits. They are the custodians and stewards of Life as it flows from the Sacred into the manifest universe.

When I attune to the stellar realm, I am attuning to this reservoir of love and energy from which Life flows, and I draw that Life into me to radiate out into my world for its benefit and that of my people. As you know, we are more beings of energy than you, and subtle energies nourish us just as physical energies nourish you. Your body forms nutrients from the sunlight it receives, and our bodies do the same from the subtle energies that flow into and through the world. We are fed by the energies of the stars which hold qualities for us that sunlight does for you. Although all Sidhe may draw on this stellar light, there are those such as myself who are able and trained to reach deeper into the stellar realms and draw forth living energies of a more powerful and pure form. What we receive, we take into ourselves and transform it into energy that all may access. This we radiate out to our world in various ways. Although you may think of me as a star priestess, I am more accurately thought of as a gatherer and conveyer of that Life that flows from cosmic sources and is the silvery blood of the cosmos, energizing all.

Interestingly, at this point in the conversation, I had a very clear image of Mariel's work. In our own case, our bodies take in sunlight and manufacture Vitamin D, among other things, and this is essential to our health. All of us can do this, and in a similar way, all Sidhe can take in subtle energies for the nourishment of their bodies. But if I put my desk lamp out into the sun and try to turn it on, nothing happens. My lamp cannot convert sunlight into energy. But if I have a solar panel in the sunlight, it can transform sunlight into electrical power that I can use to power my lamp. In a way, this is what Mariel can do. She is like a "stellar panel" transforming energies from the stellar realms into forms or frequencies those around her can take in and use.

I mentioned this to Mariel, and she laughed and offered a different metaphor, one I had used myself many times in the past (though not about the Sidhe) and which, to my chagrin as a one-time biologist, I should have thought of myself.

> **MARIEL**: I understand your image, but it is not living enough. If you would think about what I do, think instead of how your plants convert sunlight into food. It is an organic process, and so it is for me as well. I convert stellar influences into "food" for my people through the nature of who I am.
>
> In this work, much of my attunement to the stellar realm is like drinking from a pool available to all. But there are also specific stellar beings who are directly connected to the earth, to Gaia, to the Sidhe and to humanity. Think of them as the godparents of this world. They contribute to the evolution of life upon our world, including our own. Part of my work is to attune to them, both as a mediator of their energies and as an agent for their guidance.
>
> Stellar forces energize the vibrancy and flow of life within the world. At times their role is to stimulate change and to spur an evolutionary advance. They inspire new vistas of awareness and consciousness, awakening new possibilities within life. This is what is happening now to Gaia, which affects you and us as well. It is a reason there is a need to build bridges of collaboration between us.
>
> The stars are calling us all to a new way of being.

At this point, Mariel stopped with a promise to return later to continue. When she did, it was with a surprising comment.

MARIEL: Gaia is the incarnation of a star. Does this surprise you? Our Planetary Spirit is an incarnation proceeding out of the stellar realm. The stellar beings who make up this dimension of life are not individuated in the way you and I are, but they are not a single, collective consciousness either. They can individuate when needed, creating a living impulse of intent and power that can reach down into the depths of matter to create the means for Life to express in more advanced forms than that found within the substance of matter itself. Such an impulse can further individuate into what I might call a "star-soul" within whose field of life and purpose the collective intent of the stellar realm may be focused. Out of the activity of this star-soul can emerge a Planetary Spirit, such as the one ensouling our world, the one we are calling Gaia.

In this, Gaia is not so different from you or me, for our own sacred identities arise from an impulse of intent within the Sacred, and these identities in turn spawn the souls that generate our respective incarnations. The details differ, but the pattern itself is a universal one.

I spoke earlier of the two types of stellar energies to which I attune. One of these is the general field of the stellar realm as a source of Life. The other is attunement to specific stellar beings who are in relationship to this world and to the Sidhe. Included in this is a connection to the life and energies of the star-soul that is the "high self," so to speak, of Gaia. It is with these latter energies that I work most often.

"Earth energies," "solar energies," "lunar energies," and "star energies," to name four broad categories of subtle forces, are names we give to what we perceive as the sources of these phenomena, but they are not descriptions of what these energies are or what they do. I have my own experience of these energies and the differences between them, but I wished to know more what Mariel experienced and how she worked with these spiritual forces.

MARIEL: This is not easy for me to answer for I experience these forces differently than you do. Our worlds are different. We are different. I think you experience them as coming from outside yourself, but I experience them as coming from within me. The stars for you are primarily entities far distant from where you are; they are in the heavens. For me, they are woven into who I am as well as into the fabric of the world. The *anwa* of the star is part of the *anwa* of the world, as well as of ourselves. They are the stars within the earth.

Think of your parents. They are separate from you, and you can interact with them as distinct people. But they are also present in you as forces that shape your body. They are both outside you and within you. The stars are like that for me.

When I attune to a stellar being or to the stellar realms I find their resonance within me. This is the thread I follow to connect me to its source. This is like you attuning to your father by first attuning to the genes that he gave you. You find the father within you and this leads you to the father outside you. My *anwa* contains a strong stellar resonance, which allows me to do my work in the way that I do.

In making this connection, the star to whom I attune is not far distant. In a way, it is all around me. Once I find its *anwa* within me and within the world, I can blend with it and draw its qualities into my being.

You ask what the stellar energies do or what they provide. It depends. A stellar source may have a specific purpose in mind that is unique; it may, for instance, be stimulating an evolutionary quality or advance within a specific species or group. It may be stimulating evolutionary changes in Gaia itself. Remember that the stellar realms often act in a way analogous to how your soul overlights and assists your incarnated self.

To fully understand, you must understand the nature of my world and of all those who live within it. We are more material than the subtle realms but we are less material than your world. We are in many ways an energy domain. Just as different physical elements are needed to enable the functioning of your bodies and of your world as an organic whole, so we require various energetic elements or qualities. Some of these are supplied by the earth itself and by Gaia, some by the solar angels and the vast Being who is the star you know as the sun, and some by other stars and by the stellar realms altogether. All of us can absorb these energies and make them part of our world, but this process can be enhanced and empowered by people such as I. We reach directly into the pure source of these elements and draw them into our world.

Often, stellar energy stimulates the "fire," the elemental energetic force, that manifests as mind. It is not the only force that contributes to this, but it is an important one. To enrich this quality in our world is to nourish and stimulate the growth and power of our minds and their capacity to attune to the life of the cosmos. But other star sources stimulate or advance other qualities, so I cannot say to you that this is what all stellar forces do at all times in all places.

I view the stars as custodians and stewards of the evolution of life. Specific stellar beings have an interest in the development of life and consciousness within the field and *anwa* of Gaia. From time to time, they intervene. You would say they send energies that inspire and stimulate into the world; I would say they draw forth these stimulating qualities from within their *anwa* woven into the world.

It is my calling to assist this process however you may describe it.

MARIEL'S SANCTUARY

Very often when I'm in touch with Mariel, I get this same image of her in a light-filled space, receiving and absorbing sparkling energies. I thought at first what I was seeing was the room or temple in which she did her work. But it dawned on me that what I was seeing was actually an inner state of consciousness, an inner "temple," if you will.

This is something with which I have some familiarity as I have taught in my classes the creation and use of just such an inner temple, quite independently of anything to do with the Sidhe. Once I realized that this is what I was seeing, I wanted to talk to Mariel about it. This conversation arose as part of her discussion of stellar energies. I'm putting it here because I felt it deserved a chapter of its own.

> **MARIEL**: My world, like yours, is composed of living energies emerging from many sources. Some come from the stars, some from the sun, some from the moon, and some come from the earth and Gaia itself; some come from the beings of nature, and some come from humanity. Whatever their source, these energies blend together in a multitude of ways to foster the wholeness of Gaia.
>
> When I take in energies from the stars, I must welcome them within myself and help them to feel in harmony with me and my world. I invite and guide their change within myself, helping them attune to what is needed in the environment in which I am working.
>
> To do this, I must first create within myself a place of hospitality and assimilation. I call this place my Sanctuary. I create it out of who I am, out of my *anwa*, out of my nature and identity.
>
> **DAVID**: Can you describe this process?
>
> **MARIEL**: It is one with which you are familiar, but I see you are thinking about my use of the word "hospitality." As you know, subtle energies, whatever their source, are not blind and unliving as most humans would expect. They are living forces that emanate from fields of life. It is not enough simply to attune

to the stars, or the sun, or the moon. I am not a "tube" through which their energies pass. My work is to receive them lovingly and help them adapt to the world they are entering. This is what happens within my Sanctuary.

To create a Sanctuary of hospitality, I must be centered and at peace within myself, and I must be attuned to my surroundings and my world. After all, it is I, Mariel, part of the Sidhe land, who is receiving and welcoming these living emanations of stellar consciousnesses. They must know who I am if they are to begin the process of adjustment and transformation. And I must know who they are, these energies from the life of the stellar realms.

I begin this process by attuning to my own core, the knowing of who I am. This is the identity from which my *anwa* proceeds. It anchors me into myself and into my world. Think of this in this way. If you had visitors from another country come to your home to be introduced to your neighborhood, you would want your home ready to receive them and you would want to be knowledgeable about your neighborhood. You would anchor yourself in the home you have created and in your awareness of and connections with the land about you. Only if you are integrated can you help your visitors find integration.

My Sanctuary begins with my attunement to myself and then to my surroundings; in each case, what I draw forth is love: my love for who I am and my love for the world around me. My Sanctuary is built from this love, and it is this love that opens out in hospitality to the forces that are coming. After all, if I am in conflict with myself, within myself, or if I am out of harmony with the land around me, how can I provide a means for higher forces to integrate with either? How can I take them into myself? How can I give them forth to my world?

The forces I receive come out of the *anwa* of the stars, perhaps of a particular stellar being and field of life. I need to know how to attune to this. In most cases, I find this attunement in myself for the life of stars is part of my life—and your life as well. As I have said, the stars are as much within me as they are outside of me. Their life and presence is woven into my Sanctuary. If I am contacted by a stellar source with which I am unfamiliar, then I take it into myself and see how I may make it part of my life, part of my Sanctuary. Before I can receive its energies, I must receive and know its life as it resonates within me. We must together find a point of integration. This may take time.

What does it mean to process these stellar energies within me? I create in my Sanctuary a replica of the conditions with which the stellar forces are blending. There is my own identity attuned to my environment, the environment around me that is supporting my work in the place where I happen to be. This provides a basic framework and structure. Then I attune to the need or the purpose for which these stellar forces are being invited and received. What are they seeking to do in my world? What are they being asked to do? I incorporate that purpose into the field of my Sanctuary. In effect, as much as I am able, I create within myself, in my Sanctuary, a miniature of the world into which these stellar energies will be radiated. They meet my world in me.

In this process, within my Sanctuary, the stellar forces are welcomed and begin their process of attunement to my world and to how they may accomplish their purpose in my world. As this is accomplished, they are released out into my environment.

DAVID: You are doing in microcosm what you will then ask these energies to do in the macrocosm of your world. You are acclimating both them and the energies of your world together, creating a partnership. It's the quality of this partnership you then radiate. Is this correct?

MARIEL: Yes. You understand what I am seeking to explain.

It may be that my Sanctuary is held only within my own consciousness and life-field. But if more power and connection is needed, then it can expand beyond me and materialize, becoming a structure around me into which others can come if need be. It becomes a concrete place in my world for as long as it needs to be. In that state, others may join me and together we may make it a collective Sanctuary as they add their energy, their thoughts, their attunement, their *anwa* to my own. Such a building could last only as long as we need it, or it could last indefinitely even when one of us withdraws if that is the will of the group.

DAVID: This is what I have seen in visions that accompany you.

MARIEL: It is possible. You may have seen only my inner Sanctuary, for you have the sensitivity to do so. But you may have seen me and others in an externalization as well.

In addition, there are places that are consecrated for the creation of these Sanctuaries. These may be buildings or places in the landscape. In such places, the energy is built up over time to provide a serene atmosphere that supports an individual's inner work.

For this kind of work, I often find solitude a necessity. I cleanse my own energy field before beginning so that nothing will distract me as I attune to my own core and as I attune to the life seeking to enter my field. But for some of the work I do, group effort is required. Then I work in our community with others, as you have seen in the past.

DAVID: This, then, is your major work, Mariel, to provide hospitality and assimilation for stellar energies?

MARIEL: It is an important part of what I do. I also serve as a teacher and counselor when needed. In this latter work, my Sanctuary is important as well. When someone comes to me who needs help, I open the field of my Sanctuary and invite them into it. There I can take on any misaligned energies that may be in the person's field, healing them and helping the person free themselves from any ill-effect. I help them to align with their own *anwa*.

I recognize that the difference in our worlds means that I can externalize the presence of my Sanctuary in what to you would seem a concrete way. But you can create such Sanctuaries within you as well—the principles are the same for you as for me—and you can hold such a space in the etheric environment around you to embrace the energies of others. In fact, I am sure this is what good counselors in your world do instinctively. My point is that the creation of this Sanctuary is essential to my work in many ways, not only with the stars but with others whom I help.

Beyond this, much of my work now is with the calling given me by the stars, which is to enhance the connection between the worlds of the human and the Sidhe.

`The process of Sanctuary creation that Mariel describes is one with which I am familiar, at least in human terms. We each have a capacity to create such a Sanctuary or inner place of attunement, even if we are not using it to draw in subtle energies. In a manner of speaking, it is simply an extension of our own spiritual nature and its expansion into attunement with the life in the environment around us.

On another visit, Mariel described the process in more detail.

MARIEL: My Sanctuary grows out of a seed that I summon as I need it; it then unfolds in harmony with the life around me and with the life I seek to invoke and welcome.

This seed is a focus of intent drawn out of my own spiritual nature, the core of who I am. It is like a spark, a miniature star within me that represents my being's sacredness and my connection to the larger cosmos and the Spirit of the Whole. You might say I focus upon that greater identity that I am beyond my life as a Sidhe. This identity is in loving connection with the universe of life and embodies the essence of hospitality.

I then "plant" this seed into the environment around me where it expands into the Light of my Sanctuary. This is important. I could hold the seed solely in myself and allow it to expand, and if my attunement is solely for myself, this is what I would do. But I am acting as a bridge into my world. For this reason, my Sanctuary must be in resonance and partnership with my world; it must be part of my world.

DAVID: I understand. I teach a similar process I call the Grail Space. But how do you "plant" this seed?

MARIEL: I reach out to the life around me in blessing and attunement. I invite it to join me, to add its qualities and energies to mine. I then take what it offers me and draw it into my energy field to receive this seed of sacredness. As I join the two, the seed expands into a sphere that is a partnership of being and energy, containing both me and my world in a collaboration, a merging. It is this sphere that becomes my Sanctuary. It is a field of shared being, blended in love.

Into this sphere, I place another seed, this one representing that to which I am attuning, the "guest" I am inviting into my hospitality. This is not always a stellar presence. It might be an aspect of Gaia or of the earth. It might be part of the unified consciousness of the Sidhe. It depends on what the purpose of the Sanctuary is at the time I unfold it. But usually, it is a seed of star-ness.

I form this seed both from the star quality within me and within my world, as well as from the memory, held within my body, of past associations with stellar energies. Or, if I am seeking to contact that which I have never contacted before, I ask to be shown what that energy is like so I can fashion a seed from it.

This second seed is what you would call a point of resonance. It is the herald of that which I am inviting. Its purpose is to tune my Sanctuary to the appropriate presence. You would say, I believe, to the appropriate frequency, much like you tune your television or your radio. This seed is not the presence itself but the connection that will bring that presence into my Sanctuary and my Sanctuary into that presence.

I hold this second seed and attune to it, allowing it to fill my being, fill my Sanctuary. It is like gathering into a meeting place those elements that will be familiar and pleasing to my guest, as if you would prepare the favorite foodstuffs and familiar decorations in the room to which you are inviting someone from another land.

When this is done, the resonance connects us, and my Sanctuary and the presence I am contacting blend. We become one, and the work may commence between us, whatever that work may be.

When it is done, and my guest has left, I give my thanks to all who have participated. I then allow my Sanctuary to collapse back into a seed which I store as living memory within me. It then becomes a partner that I can draw one when I create a new seed and a new Sanctuary for the next time I contact this source.

DAVID: I would say, it becomes a felt sense within you, something you can always draw on.

MARIEL: Yes, it is the same, at least in principle.

In transcribing what Mariel has said here, I have drawn upon my own experiences of creating what I call a "Grail Space" to help me understand what she was describing. This is a key practice in Incarnational Spirituality, one that grew out of training I received from my original subtle world mentor, John, back in the Sixties. Simply put, he said that to connect with the subtle worlds and subtle beings, I needed to both attune to my own core identity—what I call *Sovereignty*—and to the immediate environment around me.

John was not a Sidhe but a discarnate human being. It is possible, though he never mentioned it, that he made have had his own contact with the Sidhe and that what he taught me in this regard came out of his knowledge of the practice Mariel described. However, my own experiences would suggest that this process may be a universal one precisely because it is holistic and takes into account the interconnectedness of life. That both Mariel and I use a similar method of attunement is, then, not a coincidence—or worse, a projection on my part of my process onto her—but an expression of a basic principle of working with subtle energies.

MARIEL'S CALLING

The discussions on stellar energies and Mariel's Sanctuary and work arose out of my question to her about why she was undertaking to collaborate with humans. What prompted her to do this at this time? Her answer had been that she was under instructions from a star or from the stellar realms to do so. She felt a need to explain just what those realms were to her. Having said this, there came a visit where she returned to the original question.

> **MARIEL**: You wished to know why I am doing what I am doing, seeking contact with human beings. To explain, I must tell you something of my life.
>
> Many of us do not incarnate in the same way you do; we retain a fuller connection with our core identity than is the case for most humans. You forget who you are as souls; we do not. For this reason, I remember the request I received as a soul from one of the stellar guardians of this planet to come back to be present as both our worlds—as the entirety of Gaia—goes through a time of change.
>
> Evolutionary impulses do not come as a steady impulse but in tides that ebb and flow. Likewise, there are waves that affect some parts of Gaia but not others, although what affects a part will ultimately influence the whole. As an example, an evolutionary impulse, which may come from many possible sources, may affect the consciousness and energy of the plants in the world but leave the humans unaffected, and vice versa.
>
> One of these waves was directed towards humanity over the past five hundred years. It resulted in a quickening of evolutionary development in your inner life which had consequences in the outer world. One was a movement in consciousness away from the close connections your species had had with Gaia and the realms of nature. You became more connected within yourself but less connected to your world as a living being.
>
> Now a different wave is upon us, one that seeks to renew and heighten all connections within the life-field of Gaia. It builds upon what has gone before but also seeks to correct the imbalances that have resulted, particularly within the human

sphere. Although it may not seem so to you because of our differences, in the larger view of things, we and you are both part of that sphere for we are both aspects of a greater human family and identity.

It was foreseen centuries ago that this time would come and that there would be a need for souls to take up the work of reconnection and reconciliation to promote the greater degree of wholeness now needed within Gaia. It was this foresight that led to the invitation to my soul to be one of these individuals within the realm of the Sidhe.

I was born a little over four hundred years ago, as you reckon time, in order to be ready to participate in this new developmental wave. I am young for a Sidhe, but I am old as a soul and bring much experience into incarnation with me. Since this new evolutionary wave is largely arising from stellar sources, I was born, as I described, with my *anwa* attuned to the stellar realms.

There has always been interchange between your world and mine, between the Sidhe and humans. It, too, ebbs and flows with the time and with circumstances. In recent centuries, we have drawn further apart, though there have always been individuals on both sides who have kept the connections strong. But two centuries ago, efforts began to build new bridges between us. Being young, I had only a minimal role in those efforts, which accelerated in the last century. My calling was to gather around myself a team of associates and partners who would absorb the stellar forces to which I am attuned and begin to build from them a field of energy that embodies what I might call an "*anwa* of connection." This was not as active a role as others undertook. I remained at a higher level of the Sidhe world to accomplish this, as did many of my associates. It was not my time, nor that of my association.

When it was time, I and my associates moved to where we are now, closer to your world. In this move, we have been greatly assisted by the mountain spirits to which we attune and which form a backdrop to our location. The city already existed, as I have described, but our own community and dwellings came into being after our move.

There are many groups such as ours around the world, as well as individuals within the Sidhe, who are part of this new wave of connection and reconciliation. We are exploring many strategies of contact and cooperation. The card deck we created with you is one such strategy, but by no means the only one. This is a joyful and exciting time for us and one of challenge as well, for there is not much we can do without your collaboration. Finding the proper gateways into your imaginations, your minds, and your hearts, and thus into your activities, is not a simple nor an easy process. There is much disbelief and misconception around who and what we are in your world. Like the salmon, we must swim upstream against strong currents of negativity, but we are strong. We will reach the place where we can spawn a new world together.

DAVID: Why did you come to me specifically? There are others who have had longer and deeper associations with the Sidhe than I and who are already working to promote contact and collaboration. I had no contact with you at all until you came.

MARIEL: It was not by chance. Though you may not remember it, we made contact before you incarnated. We are not unknown to each other. And the fact that you had no preconceptions about us was an advantage, allowing us to start from scratch, as you would say. The main reason, however, is that the work you and your colleagues are doing with the mysteries and power of incarnation is important to us as well and creates a resonance between us. We seek to further the incarnation of Gaia, do we not? Shared goals create bridges, and I crossed over the one you and your associates were and are making.

I was thinking about the work that Mariel and her associates—and other Sidhe around the world—are doing to connect with human beings. Important as it is, and delightful as the contact is for those who have it, it did not seem like very much or that it could make a significant difference. A couple of thousand people might use the *Card Deck of the Sidhe* to have a contact of some nature with the Sidhe, but in a world population approaching eight billion, that's not even a drop in a bucket. This doesn't consider the challenges to wholeness and a shared understanding created by all the cultural, linguistic, ethnic, and racial differences that divide humanity. When next Mariel visited, I put my doubts to her.

DAVID: As much as I appreciate the work we're doing together and honor what we've achieved, it's a very small pebble dropped into an enormously large lake. Very few will be affected by the ripples or even see them.

MARIEL: Never underestimate the effect of small stones. Dropped in the right place at the right time, they can cause avalanches.

DAVID: I agree. And I don't mean to imply any lack of hope. I'm very hopeful and positive about what can be achieved. Still, I want to be realistic and not have unreasonable expectations or projections about our work. That, I feel, would be unhealthy and counterproductive.

MARIEL: Yes. This is true. If our strategy were only to offer information about us through books and cards, then you would be correct. This will reach only a few people among your many millions. However, there is more to what we are doing than meets the eye. Remember that, compared to you, we are beings of thought and energy, which gives us ways of affecting the inner life of humanity beyond what appears on the surface.

DAVID: You can influence how people think….

MARIEL: Not in the way you are imagining. We must also respect the sovereignty of individuals. It is not our strategy to manipulate. However, those of us who are called to this work of reconciliation, contact, and collaboration have been working for some time now to create an energetic field that can affect the collective energy field of humanity, or at least significant parts of it. Think of it as a bubble pressing against the membrane of another bubble, nudging it to move in a particular direction. We are "leaning in" to press against the human energy field with the strength and vision of our own. We are adding our presence and "weight," so to speak, to all the other subtle and spiritual forces now acting upon humanity to effect change.

People may not at all be aware of our presence, nor need they be, but there will be a steady momentum growing towards actions and choices that will benefit all our world. There is resistance as well. We cannot interfere with the freedom of humanity to shape its own destiny, but we can persuade by our energetic presence.

Understand that this presence is not channeled through a single individual such as myself or any other Sidhe, no matter how developed she or he may be. It is a collective influence, a push from our species upon your species. But there are those of us who focus this push and help provide contact between the two energy fields.

Not all Sidhe are behind this. As I have said in the past, there are those among us who wish nothing to do with humanity, and for most of us, contact with your collective energy field is difficult and at times painful. But those of us who are called to this work form a buffer. We draw as much of the collective attention and energy of the Sidhe as we can towards this effort, and we support each other in ways that make contact with you less challenging. We are dedicated and trained for this work of connection.

Part of my work with the stellar energies is to draw their strength and assistance into this field of contact. This empowers all of us who are part of it and can draw upon it to work in contact with your human energies.

DAVID: Are our energies so very painful, then?

MARIEL: At times. It depends on circumstances, on where the contact is being made, and on what is happening in your world. As I said in one of our first conversations, we draw upon your joy, your strength, your stability and balance to augment our own. The energy environment may be difficult at one time and in one place, but the person we are contacting can more than make up for this if he or she is generating positive qualities of mind and heart.

Also, we draw upon the forces of nature and of the earth for assistance. In your area, I draw upon the presence and energy of the mountains and of the forests which are plentiful. There are many Sidhe who have a deep attunement to the natural energies and to the nature spirits of a region who are aided by this in their contact with humans.

The field I and my associates help to generate is a field of contact that focuses the collective presence and qualities of the Sidhe into a form that can affect and nudge human energy and consciousness. Sidhe have been in contact with humanity for millennia, as I have said, but this field creates a new channel through which this can take place, one tailored for this time in history.

The images that came to me while Mariel was describing this were interesting. The main one was of a collective force being created to affect the mental and emotional energies of human beings. Mariel spoke of "nudging," but this "nudge" was not so much one of pressure as it was of presence. That is, the more energy went into this field, the more presence it had, and this presence was acting in what I can only call an inspirational (or maybe a charismatic) way. There was no sense of coercion at all. Rather, there was a strong element of suggestion. Or put another way, the presence of this Sidhe-created "field of reconciliation and connection" was like an "attractor" in chaos theory, enhancing the probability that events could move in a desired direction.

The next time I connected to Mariel, I asked her for more information about this.

MARIEL: Please understand that I and my associates are not trying to move humanity in a direction of our choosing. This is not our calling. We are creating a presence out of our own beingness that holds the possibility of wholeness and connectedness. By holding this strongly in proximity to the energy field of humanity, individual human beings feel it and begin to react, some by moving towards that possibility and others by resisting it. But moving towards wholeness does not dictate the path you will take or what forms that wholeness may take as you learn to manifest it. We are not determining the shape of your future, but we are opening pathways for you to do so in greater understanding of how interconnected and dependent we all are upon each other. We are opening pathways for you to understand that you live embedded in and part of a community of life, not in a world filled with inert and dead objects for you to manipulate. We are opening pathways for you to understand the realms of living energies and the power of imagination, thought, and love in collaborating with the same. How you walk these pathways, or even if you set foot upon them at all, is your choice. We cannot make you live up to your potentials, nor can you do this for us. This is something we must do together in mutual assistance.

There was more that Mariel had to say concerning the engagement of the Sidhe with humanity, but I am saving those conversations for the following chapter as it seemed better to highlight them on their own. There was one other conversation, though, in which Mariel discussed her calling and her work with me on the card deck, and by implication, the work of other Sidhe engaged in working with human individuals.

MARIEL: Do not minimize the value of the card deck we created, nor those other contacts with human beings which have resulted in books being written. Information about us and offering means for humans to contact with our energy and presence all serve the same purpose as our collective field. We need connections with you to draw our field closer to humanity and to bind it to your world. Every contact, however minor it may seem, helps. For this purpose, we do not need to connect with a great many people. If you honor the connections you have and draw us close in partnership, it helps our whole field come closer.

Think of the card deck and the books as hooks you place in a great cliff that you are scaling. The hooks don't make the cliff smaller, but they give a means for you and us to connect to the mountain side. They make the climb easier.

My calling is to call the field of connection into being and to nourish it with the energies I can call forth. Within this calling, though, the work we do through the cards and the books are an extra joy, and when people use them, the value to us that results should not be underestimated.

I thought that Mariel had said all she was going to say about her work and her calling, but early one morning, I awakened to feeling her presence in my mind. "This is one other thing I wish to say," she said. So, I got up and transcribed the following.

MARIEL: In our earlier discussions [*recorded in* Conversations with the Sidhe—*David*], we talked at length about the split between our two peoples. This also is part of my calling, to heal this division. To this end, I often travel to meet with those of my kind who do not trust humans and wish little or nothing to do with you. The split must be healed from both sides; reconciliation is not simply a human challenge.

However, I also do not want to lay too much emphasis upon this split, for it is not the only defining feature of the Sidhe/human relationship.

DAVID: Can you explain more about this? I've had the feeling, too, that defining our people and our relationship solely in terms of a split that occurred over the matter of incarnation is too limiting. It doesn't tell the whole picture.

MARIEL: You are correct. Let me tell you some of our history. First, though, I must tell you my understanding of physical matter and the world in which you live. The physical realm is one form of emanation of the cosmos; it existed long before Gaia came into being or descended from its stellar home. Though it is living, it did not initially produce or sustain life. Do you understand? It provides a specialized form of consciousness that is important to the Sacred. I cannot explain it, for I do not fully understand it, but let us say it provides an anchor that allows creation to unfold on multiple levels of being and consciousness.

The strength of this consciousness and the realm that proceeds from it is based on its limits and its focus. Aeons ago, again long before Gaia came into being, there were those who felt these limits and their focus could be used to accelerate the development of life and consciousness. Efforts were made to bring life into these realms. Most of these efforts stopped short of a full immersion into the most focused manifestation of this consciousness of matter, but some determined to quicken the life within matter and give it a power of emergence and evolution. Ultimately, Gaia was one of these beings who pledged to bring life into the cosmos in order that new life might emerge out of it.

In time, that collective field of souls that are the ancestors of all that is human and Sidhe joined in this effort. Many of these souls agreed to enter into the depths of matter to serve the arising and quickening of life. You must understand that to these beings, this was not a descent into form or substance; this they already possessed in their own way. It was a taking on of a specialized, limited form of consciousness to expand it from within. You would see this as entering into matter.

It was decided that there would be those who would go to the threshold of this consciousness but no further in order to be a lifeline for those who went deeper. This was their mission and calling, and there was no rejection or refusal on their part of matter or its consciousness and life.

Of those who consented to go fully into limitation, there came a point where some of them stopped and refused to go further. This is when the "split" took place. Part of this split was a considered one, a realization that much might be lost in this new state of consciousness and that perhaps the decision to enter it should be more carefully examined. These were beings who didn't back away out of rejection but out of a sense of caution. But others became fearful and simply refused to continue. Both these groups formed what now are the Sidhe. They became caught in a half-way place, not willing to go forward but unable to go back; this half-way place became the Sidhe world. It is a "half-physical" incarnation.

I did not originate with the Sidhe world. I was one of those who formed part of the life-line, those who never intended to go fully into matter and thus did not participate in the split. But to do the work to which I am called, I have taken form and life within the world of the Sidhe who did split away from the original intent.

DAVID: So you are a bridge not only between the Sidhe and humanity but between one branch of the Sidhe and another?

MARIEL: Yes, this is so.

I tell you this so you realize the story of the split between our people is not the whole story. There are Sidhe who were never participants in that split and who still hold in themselves the original unity of Sidhe and Human.

This means that there are resources of wholeness and connection upon which both of us, Sidhe and embodied human, may draw that hold us in communion, hold us in connection and togetherness, hold us in a field in which reconciliation and healing may take place. It is my calling to make those resources available as fully as I can.

ENGAGING HUMANITY

As we move further into the 21st Century, humanity is facing a growing list of problems, most of its own making. We are a species struggling to change and resisting it at the same time. While there is no question we need to deal with the consequences of our own beliefs and actions, it is also true that we are receiving help from many sources, the Sidhe being one. I wanted to explore with Mariel just what the help from the Sidhe might look like and how they are engaging humanity, particularly in light of what she has said about her calling.

MARIEL: As I have said, my people have dealt with physical humanity for millennia in a variety of ways, but now we are learning to engage with you in new ways. In this, we are learning as well, so you must consider our efforts to be, as you would say, a "work in progress."

In our conversations, we speak as if there were one humanity, but there is not. Humanity exists on different layers, as do we. The most comprehensive and inclusive of these layers, aside from the soul of humanity itself, is a collective planetary energy field that embraces all physical human beings. But as we move "downward," so to speak, towards the realms of specific human nations and groups, as well as individuals, this field breaks up into many lesser fields, between which there can be conflict and turmoil. It is this that makes it difficult for us to work with you at too close a level. There are human fields that are compatible with our own and open to us, and there are human fields that are antagonistic.

DAVID: When you talk about these smaller fields, you are talking about nations and societies, or smaller groups? Races? Religions?

MARIEL: Yes, in part. Every individual, every group of any size generates a field of living energy. I am thinking of those large collectives that both divide and define humanity and prevent you from seeing yourselves and acting as a single planetary species. My point is simply that if we work with humanity as a whole, it is at a level removed from your everyday activity and thinking. If we work closer to the ground, so to speak, then we must work with these smaller fields which are diverse and often in conflict. So we must choose those that are amenable and open to our influence. This can vary from place to place and even from one time to another depending on what is happening in the minds and hearts of those creating those fields.

DAVID: This is more complex than I was imagining.

MARIEL: There are four broad strokes to how we engage with you. We work with the collective human field, which itself is attempting to impress its inclusiveness and connectedness into the consciousness and activity of the lesser fields within it.

DAVID: And this large collective field is not the soul of humanity?

MARIEL: No. It is the unified field of your incarnate species. It is linked to the soul of humanity, but they are not identical. Then, where possible, we work with those lesser fields that are open to us and to our influence. As I said, this may vary and change over time and place depending on the people who are part of the field.

Though we can work with large fields of energy, such as those generated by a nation, we generally do not. There are other Beings who do that work. We work with smaller groups that are more identified with specific places in the land. Although we are not spirits of nature, we are attuned to and often shaped by influences arising from the land, as I have described. We can thus work more easily with a group whose identity and field of energy also are tied to the land in some fashion.

Our third strategy is to work with individuals, such as yourself. Partnerships we form with individuals can in turn strengthen our links with the larger fields of which these individuals are a part. With individuals, our work can also be specific, which is usually not possible when we work with the larger collective fields of energy and life.

Our fourth strategy is to work with the land itself, with the forces of nature, and with Gaia. This may seem to have little to do with humanity, but you are also part of the land, part of Gaia. We work where and as we can to counteract some of the negative impacts you are creating, but there are others among the spirits and angels of nature who do this as well and often better than we can. What we can do is reach to the deep layers of your humanity through the land to which you are also attuned, whether you are conscious of it or not. For all your achievements in separating yourselves, you are still part of the planet. We can reach into your energy through those ancient links.

DAVID: You connect with humanity in diverse ways, then. What is the work you do with us through these connections, broadly speaking?

MARIEL: First, it must be clear that we cannot meet all your needs. We are not your spiritual teachers. We are your evolutionary kin; we are bonded on a shared evolutionary journey of service to the life of Gaia. So much of what we offer takes the form of calling you back to this bond and to this service. But I know you are wishing a more specific answer. You realize that the specifics of how the Sidhe interact with human beings depends on circumstances and on the parties involved. With you, for instance, our engagement and help has taken the form of cards and books! Certainly, not every Sidhe who contacts a human is doing so out of dedication to a larger planetary service or on behalf of reconciliation. Some are simply curious or are being adventurous. Some are guardians of specific landscapes into which humans may have wandered. Some may have their own personal motivations.

There are individual Sidhe who may wish to partner with you to help with your endeavors and activities and in the process, learning more about the human world and your incarnational nature. Not all Sidhe are as skilled at this as others, but as much as possible, they tailor their approach to you to conform to your individual characteristics and surroundings. They certainly carry forward the process of reconciliation and blending, but this may not be their overarching motive, you understand? They may be genuinely motivated by a desire to help but also by a desire to learn and to grow in their own understanding. After all, your world in many ways is as wondrous, mysterious, and magical to us as our world is to you.

You have asked what help the Sidhe can give to humanity. One form of help is what we are doing here and what others of my kind are doing with others of your kind. This is to provide information about us and to trigger a memory in people of being part of a much larger world than their senses may reveal to them. We can encourage you to think of your connections to Gaia, to nature, and to each other. It's important to remember your larger self and its connections.

There is much that you need that we cannot provide or that is provided by other sources such as your allies in the subtle realms. But what we see is that you become entangled in webs of thought and feeling that limit your ability to act from your fullest potential. Remember who we are. We are the people of peace for whom joy and connectedness are second nature. Many of you may feel that such qualities are of little use in meeting the challenges you face or the conflicts and suffering of your world. But you live lives of stress that bind your energy and make you more likely just to react than to act with awareness. If you could think and feel less defensively, with greater calm and with joy, then you would more easily find the natural sources of insight and wisdom that exist within you. Drawing on such innate sources could guide your thinking, your feeling, and your actions, giving you greater ability to meet and solve your problems.

You have answers to your problems, but in your distress and fear, anger and agitation, you do not see them or are unwilling to accept them. We cannot make you see or accept those answers, but we can be a presence of joy and peace around you that gives you a chance to alter your inner environment to where the answers arise within you with conviction.

Yes, there are times when we can act directly upon the natural environment around you to bring healing, though again we do so in conjunction with other forces. Yes, there are times we can, when you are open and hospitable to us, work with you as individuals to make positive changes more likely in your lives. But we do not do these things through magic. We do them by, as I have said, "leaning into" you and sharing our presence with you in ways that draw forth its equivalence within you. After all, you, too, are fundamentally beings of peace, of joy, of love, and of connection. These qualities may be much layered over by what you accumulate in your lives, but they are there nonetheless. We can, if given the opportunity, help you to draw them forth. This is what it means to find your "Sidhe within."

Humans take drugs to feel calm, to feel peace, to feel joy, and to enhance their performance. In so doing, you can miss seeing the sources of these strengths that exist within you. We are not drugs for you, but we can help quicken your awareness of your own inner resources. Attune to us, and we can help bring you to the realizations and harmony that you now achieve imperfectly and in limited ways with your chemicals.

In other words, we cannot solve humanity's problems. They are long in the making and rest upon your shoulders. But we can make that burden lighter and we can help you help yourselves by finding your own powers of joy and peace, connectedness and wholeness. We can offer you the resonance of our own nature, sounding a note that can draw forth its answering response within you. Then, together, we bring harmony to the world.

DAVID: And what do the Sidhe get in return from working with humanity?

MARIEL: Individual Sidhe may satisfy their curiosity about you and your world; they may gain pleasure from working with a human, both from giving aid and from learning about you. It depends on the motive of the Sidhe who is engaging with you. Some simply have pleasure in the contact.

I cannot answer this for all the Sidhe, for all the Sidhe are not engaging with you. However, because we are sensitive to the well-being and wholeness of Gaia, any way that your respond to our influence and presence that leads you to be more harmoniously connected to the world will benefit us. After all, wholeness benefits us all. We have no desire to see the world descend into greater brokenness and destruction, with ever greater loss of life. Even if we are not directly endangered, it diminishes us just as it diminishes humanity.

There is another benefit. It is a matter of *anwa*. As we have said, we come from a common ancestor. Because of this, in the beginning of our relationship with Gaia, we had a collective *anwa*. We are two separate groups now, each with our own *anwa*, but we are both still part of that ancient source and field of life. We still share the original *anwa*. When we are able to work and commune together, we are repairing the *anwa* that was broken. Until this is fully done, neither you nor we can fully live up to those innate potentials that arise from our collective origin and our collective wholeness.

You are the ones who descended into the fullness of matter, we are the ones who remained behind. You are learning what is there in the depths of physical incarnation, knowledge we do not have. We have knowledge of what you left behind. Together, when our experience and knowledge is combined, we gain deeper insight and wisdom into the planet as a whole, as well as into who we both are in our full nature.

You are masters of incarnation in ways that we are not, so when we associate with you, we can learn what you have learned. We are masters of joy and connectedness and of the powers of seeing and creating wholeness. When we associate, it can awaken these skills in you, which, when applied, will benefit us both.

More than this, I cannot say. We will need to see what emerges for both our peoples to fully know what we give to each other. We are only in the time of first steps, and much has yet to be revealed to us both.

The issue of climate change and the impact humanity is having on the environment is a major and growing concern to many people. It is on track to become the number one challenge we will face in the world. I wanted to know what Mariel's thoughts were on this and how, if at all, the Sidhe might be able to help. During one of our contacts, I asked her.

DAVID: Human activity is having an adverse impact upon the world, as evidenced in climate change. Are you aware of this?

Are you affected by it? Is this something you can help with?

MARIEL: We are aware, yes, and we are affected by it. Changes in the earth, in weather and land formation, can have effects in those parts of our world that touch or are close to yours. Imbalances within Gaia's system can cause us to withdraw even further to protect our own world. Connection between our worlds becomes harder as many Sidhe retreat away from human engagement. There are secondary effects as well. As the human emotional and thought realms become even more agitated with fear and suffering, it is harder for those of us dedicated now to reconciling our worlds to come into your energy fields. For those of you wishing to work with us, I am not saying you should not be concerned with what is happening, but it is even more important that you find a calm center that can build a stable platform of contact for both of us.

Can we help? Our ability to do so is limited. This is a humanly created problem, and the solutions lie with you. It's not as if many humans do not know what to do or what is needed. What is lacking is an alignment of thought and a clear intention to address the problem and serve the well-being of all life on your world, or at the very least, to protect your own lives by taking appropriate actions.

We can assist, as I mentioned before, by bringing our energetic presence to bear upon your collective energy field in ways that can inspire new thought and vision as well as the will to become a guardian species for the world. We can work with individuals who open to us to empower their ability to act and choose in ways that benefit your world.

There are Sidhe who are attuned to the spirits of nature who are working to assist. Many of these spirits are now out of balance and agitated as the interconnections of the world are changed or disrupted. The Sidhe who are able seek to calm and balance them. This by itself cannot stop the changes that are upon you, but it can channel otherwise destructive energies in less harmful ways. But here, too, we are limited. We are not spirits of nature ourselves, as I have said. True help must come from other sources, from the great angels and Devas that overlight the patterns of nature. But to secure their help, you must come into alignment with them, and this means coming into alignment with the good of all life.

We do all that we can, but it's in partnership alone that the true solutions to this problem will come. Your people must learn that you are not alone or supreme upon this world. You must find your partnership with the life around you, whether its physical life, subtle life, spiritual life, or Sidhe life. You are part of a vast ecology; it is your ignorance and forgetfulness of this fact that is creating danger and disaster for you. Remember your connections. If we, the Sidhe, can help you to do this and to act upon that remembrance, then we will be joyous indeed.

In my own interaction with the Sidhe, I view them as friends and at times, as with Mariel, as co-workers, rather than as spiritual teachers or guides. Mariel has been clear that she does not see herself as a "spiritual ally" and leaves that role to others who operate out of the spiritual and subtle realms, as I describe in my book *Subtle Realms: An Explorer's Field Notes*. Figuring that they have more important things to do than be involved in my daily life, I rarely reach out to them for assistance.

There have been times, however, when they have been helpful, usually if I'm doing a form of subtle energy work like subtle activism or manifestation. I describe this kind of work in *Working with Subtle Energies*, and if I ask their help, I have found the Sidhe to be willing and gracious in adding their energy to my own. Mariel speaks of their "leaning in," and I have personal experience of how this can be of assistance. I have felt my own energy field being enhanced by their presence, like getting a "booster shot."

Sometimes it is Mariel who will provide this assistance, but knowing how busy she is, I am reluctant to bother her except for a project like working on this book of new conversations. However, there is another Sidhe, a male, who seems to have less trouble operating within the "close-in" energy fields of the physical plane and who is the one who usually assists me if I ask for their help. I have invited him to participate in these conversations, but he declined, saying simply that he was not "a speaker" and did not wish to intrude. Perhaps I'll be able to persuade him differently in the future.

We all have spiritual allies whose role it is to help us with our incarnations. Their presence is often symbolized in the concept of "guardian angels." The Sidhe are not these beings.

A couple of days after I had the conversation I recorded above, Mariel came back with further thoughts, not about climate change but about the relationship of the Sidhe to humanity.

> **MARIEL**: I have said some of this previously, but I wish to make it clear. When it comes to engaging with humanity, the Sidhe are not all of one mind. There are Sidhe who wish nothing to do with you at all. There are Sidhe who cannot deal with you in your current state, even if they wished. They are too far removed from the human and physical vibrational domains and cannot re-enter them. There are Sidhe who are undecided and who are observing. They can be engaged, but they are suspicious and cautious, for reasons embedded in our joint history as well as in how you are behaving towards the earth at this time. However, if pathways are opened to them through your own hospitable hearts, they can respond. They bear you no ill-will, but your ways of thinking are alien to them and hurtful; they do not know how much they can trust you.
>
> Then there are those like myself who know we must work together for a common future. We look for all the avenues that can open for us to link with you, engage with you, and cooperate with you for the good of Gaia. And for your own good, as well, for we would see you open to your larger self, to the joy and wonder that lies within you. We do not wish simply to help you but to dance with you. For that to happen, you must hear the music as we do and recover the suppleness of being that is part of your nature.
>
> What you must realize is that we are learning, too. Engaging with you as we are doing is new to many of us, even though we have been preparing for it. We are not always sure of the best ways to proceed. So much is in flux for your people and for mine, as it is for the earth itself. We are feeling our way, even as you are. But as more of us on both sides make the effort to connect, the more understanding grows and pathways of service and collaboration emerge.
>
> I have told you in the past that our people and yours used to

meet in special places, gathering in circles to mingle our energies and bless the earth. Many of the stone circles in your world hold the memory of this, but in the beginning, there were no stones, only those who stood and held the communal space. The card deck that I gave you connects to those ancient circles and to the energies of connectedness and blessing.

We still hold these gatherings in our world but linked to places in yours, usually deep in wilderness, where human energies are faint. Where humans make it possible through their connectedness with us, we can link to places closer to humankind as well. In these gatherings, those of us come together who have taken on mantles as guardians not only of the earth but of our connectedness as well, guardians of the ancient spirit of Humanity as well as of the Humanity to come. We join our forces to bless the earth, bless humankind, and bless Gaia. We channel the energies of the stars. We open the ancient cauldrons of emergent life and wonderment. We dance the dances of joy and hope. We celebrate life and give the blessing of this appreciation and honoring of life back to the world.

You can always join us in your heart and in your imagination. Take up a mantle as guardian of life and let joy be your solid core, hope the fire within you, and love the gift you offer those around you. We seek to make the Earth itself our gathering, and all people our standing stones. You can share this vision with us and keep it in your heart. Then we are truly engaging in a work of healing and reconciliation.

The concept of joy is one that often arose in these conversations, not always explicitly but implied. Mariel is a joyous being; joy pours out from her as a natural radiance. Nor is she alone in this. It seems a quality inherent in all the Sidhe that I have met. Whether this is a universal quality for all Sidhe everywhere, I have no idea, but it has certainly been a constant with the ones I have come to know.

In talking about their relationship with humanity, the subject of joy came up in an explicit way.

MARIEL: I have said that we "lean in" to you with our energy, using our collective presence to influence where possible your own human fields of thought and feeling. In particular, we seek to share and inspire the quality of joy.

DAVID: This is something I always feel in your presence.

MARIEL: Yes, it is part of who we are. But do you understand and experience it as we do? Joy for us is not an emotion of happiness but a relationship we have with what might be called the "energies of life." Joy enhances and at times even makes possible flow and connection.

DAVID: The image I get as you say this is that of a lubricant. It's as if joy were something that greases the gears, so to speak, making them work better and more smoothly.

MARIEL: Yes, you get the sense of what I am trying to convey. It is not something we feel in response to good things happening in our lives. It is a quality we generate to add to life. Where there is joy, all other energies flow more gracefully and powerfully. Thought is enhanced. Feeling is enhanced. Presence is enhanced.
When we "lean into you," we offer our joy to so that you may take it into yourselves and act with greater connectedness and wisdom. Your challenge is that your connections with the world and with each other are broken. Joy can help you mend this.

DAVID: Most people, I think, would look at the state of humanity and of the world and not feel joyous. In fact, people can get angry with those who feel joy, feeling they are not serious enough or grounded enough. How can you be joyous, they ask, when there is so much suffering, so much pain, so much anger and evil in the world?

MARIEL: I understand. But I would simply repeat that this is a mistaken understanding of what joy is. You confuse it with happiness or pleasure, with things going as you want them to. It is a reaction. For us, it is an action. It is a gift. It is a flowing out of who we are. It is a recognition that if we wish life to go smoothly and if we wish to be as connected as possible, we must do something to allow this. What we do is joy.

This is not just a Sidhe ability. It is your ability, too. It comes from a loving heart. You need to change your thinking about the nature of joy, and perhaps my words will help in this regard. We do not wish you to deny or overlook the darkness and brokenness in your world. Joy isn't a turning away of your vision to see only what is pleasing and beautiful. Joy is a power, perhaps second only to love.

Love defines and shapes the path forward, hope opens the gates to take that path, and joy strengthens and empowers your walking. None of these things are emotions alone, certainly not in the simple way you define emotions. They are powers. They govern how things proceed, how things act. They affect the probability of connection and the likelihood of graceful flow and exchange. They make life possible.

Do not underestimate joy nor deny it in the face of evil. Joy is the fire of fiery hope; it is the power you need to confront the darkness coming to the surface in your world.

We are joy because we choose to be. We choose to generate it. This is a choice you can make, too. It is a choice not of how you will see your world but of how you will see yourself and your own capabilities.

MAKING CONTACT

In our conversation about engaging with human beings, Mariel discussed ways of making contact.

MARIEL: We contact and communicate with you in three ways. The first is through telepathy. This can be used by a Sidhe who is familiar with your human ways of thinking. The second is through the heart, a form of empathetic connection based on feelings. The third is through a blending of energy fields. The latter can contain telepathic and empathetic elements but it is based on a more intimate sharing of life-force and being.

Each of these has its appropriate uses and its pros and cons. Telepathic contact, for us, is the most limited. In our own communication with each other, we do not use words in the same way or to the same extent that you do. We communicate with each other through symbols and glyphs of meaning. Engaging with you telepathically often requires that we think in your languages, though we can transmit images as well. This is not always easy for us to do as we must think and craft our messages more slowly than is normal for us. We are also dependent on the mental ability and content of the individual since we often draw upon your vocabulary and store of images and concepts to express ourselves in ways you can understand. The richer and more agile the human mind, the richer our communication can be.

However, telepathy has two advantages for us. The first is that through it we can communicate with you at a distance. If a mental link is established, we do not have to enter the energy field of the material world to be in telepathic contact. If you will pardon the analogy, at times this is like being able to telephone someone in a war zone without having to enter that war zone ourselves.

The second advantage relates to the other two modes of communication. Let me explain them first, then I will return to what telepathy offers us.

The second form of contact is through your heart and your feelings. It is a form of empathetic communication. This has an advantage in that we can often convey more through your feeling nature than we can through your mind. Your mind may be locked into habits of thought that can obstruct what we wish to say, whereas your feelings are more fluid and open. They can expand to take in the full quality of what we wish to say. Of course, this is not always the case, for your emotional nature can become hardened and difficult to penetrate as well. But it is quite likely that your first intimation of us, your initial contact, will be through what you *feel* rather than through what you *think*.

As with telepathy, this mode of communication has disadvantages as well as advantages. Your emotional life can be tumultuous by our standards; trying to reach you through your feelings can be like trying to cross a stormy sea. We may think we have established a clear message and then something can cause you to change your emotional state, and it will be lost or distorted.

Like telepathy, though, one of the main advantages of connecting with you through your heart and your feelings is how it can make possible the third mode of contact, that of energy to energy, life-field to life-field, being-to-being.

This third mode can be the most difficult. It is a matter of our *anwa* blending with your *anwa*, our song of being blending with your song of being so that we sing in tandem. When this is achieved, as you know, we become each other, and that which we wish to communicate with you becomes part of your whole experience, not just a thought or a feeling, though both may be present.

This is our preferred mode of communication, but it is challenging. Because you have training in using your energy field as a mode of communion and communication, it is easier to blend with you than it might be with someone for whom the whole concept is a difficult one, much less its execution. Still, even for you, it has not been easy. As you have experienced, our energy fields are very different, though this depends on the nature of the Sidhe who is contacting you. I am not one who normally lives near or works with the vibrations of the earth, therefore my energy field was less suited than some for the work we have undertaken. I have associates who are more skilled in this area than I, and I may send one of them to you in the future. On the other hand, because of my work, I have insights that others of my companions may not have. Further, as one of the instigators and holders of this project in which we are engaged together, it's important that I participate when I can.

It's in this area of blending our energy fields that telepathy and empathy can play an important role. When you think of us and form an image in your mind, that image, even if imperfect, can provide an initial link with you. This image can be of us or it could be a symbolic image, such as the glyph provided by others of my kind to your colleague or the images we presented in the card deck of our co-creation. This image can then connect to and expand within your feeling nature. The image may inspire feelings of joy or love with which we can align and which draw us closer to you. In this way, the door into your energy field may open.

The challenge is if the image begins to obstruct by insisting on its veracity and existence, for then rather than being a point of contact, it becomes obstructive. You experienced this when you imaged me as a woman. This was a helpful image to the extent that it represented who I am, but the more the image became a human one, the less flexibility it had and the more it got in the way of our connection.

The same is true when it is your feelings that provide a road into your being. It is one thing to hold a quality of love and joy; we can resonate with these. But a human's feelings can become focused upon their own needs and become demanding energetically. A person may draw self-importance from the contact with us, using us to satisfy a need in themselves.

Another disadvantage to the third mode of contact, the blending of our energy and beingness, is that we must be close to you for this to occur. We need to enter your incarnate energy field, or draw you into our world energetically. This requires greater exertion on our part. In my own case, as you know, I was accompanied for the first few times I came into your world by two of my associates who provided strength and stability for our energy fields. But once you and I established this blending, then I can now draw on your strength to be present.

Here are my recommendations for connecting with us. Hold a mental image of us that is clear and consistent but flexible at the same time, an image that helps you feel in touch with us but which you are willing to change or let go of. Hold qualities of strength and calm, joy and love, and peace as you think of us. Welcome us emotionally and with hospitality in your heart. The more serene and welcoming your emotional field is, the easier it is for us to connect with you. Invite us into your world and into your life with a willingness that we may both benefit from the contact. Be still and allow our beings to touch and blend as much as is appropriate for both of us. Feel us in your body as well as in your mind and heart. Feel us in your surroundings, blessing the space around you even as you bless it. Then we feel the chances are enhanced for communication.
Blessings!

Over the past decade, I've been asked many times, "How might I contact the Sidhe?" In some ways, I'm the wrong person to ask since I never set out to contact them myself. They took the initiative, and it happened. I imagine the reason they did so is because I've been working collaboratively with subtle beings for over sixty years using methods very like what Mariel described. Whatever the reason, the fact is that I did not use a method to make a contact, so I have no experience that way to draw upon in giving someone else advice. What I can say is that my friend and colleague John Matthews offers a technique in his book *The Sidhe* using a glyph as a mental image for a point of contact. And the *Card Deck of the Sidhe* was specifically designed to facilitate contact by providing both mental and emotional content in the form of evocative images within a definite mental structure. Both John's approach and the card deck work with the ideas that Mariel has put forth, so they are worth a look if you are interested. I would add that John himself has just produced a new Sidhe-inspired card deck called *The Moon Oracle of the Sidhe*, so it's not as if individuals within the Sidhe are not working to provide us with tools.

The most basic principle of contact is that of affinity. Put bluntly, to contact a Sidhe, be like a Sidhe. Share their concerns for the well-being of life, be a source of peace and joy in your life, find ways to serve our world. After all, one way to bring musicians into your life is to start playing music.

In *Conversations with the Sidhe*, I presented an exercise which was originally inspired by Mariel. It was not intended, in the way the card deck was, as a way of contacting the Sidhe. Its intent is for a person to step into a role that a Sidhe would take on, thereby becoming "Sidhe-like" in relationship to service to Gaia. It's not really an exercise at all but a covenant, a form of initiation and commitment. As with all such things, a person needs to be willing to enter such a covenant and initiation; it can never be forced. And for it to "take," it must be entered into in right timing when a person is ready for its implications and consequences and with a spirit that understands what it is taking on. I called it the Guardian Mantle Exercise, and I repeat it here.

THE GUARDIAN MANTLE EXERCISE

If you have a Sidhe Card Deck, keep it handy, but don't use it to begin with. Its use comes later in the exercise. If you don't have a Sidhe Card Deck, you can do all the steps perfectly well in your imagination.

You begin by imagining yourself in front of an ancient stone circle, one that is rooted deep in the earth, the stones covered with moss and faint carvings. You can feel an energy radiating from it. Just as if you were going to enter someone's home, identify yourself and ask permission to step into the circle. Wait just a moment in silence, allowing yourself to be seen. The permission is granted.

Step into the Circle. As you stand within it, surrounded by the presence of these ancient stones, it feels like you are in a great Cauldron held by Gaia, the Soul of the world. Into this space have poured over the centuries energies of consciousness and life brought into this world across the threshold of this Circle from sources distant and near: from stars, from the sun and moon, and from the deep fires of life within the heart of the earth. Here these forces are synthesized, blended into a wholeness and shared with the world.

Although the Cauldron is empty as you stand in it, you can sense the power of holding within this place. You can feel a Grail in your own heart and life—your own powers of holding—resonating with it. Take a moment just to go deeply into the felt sense of this Circle Cauldron.

Behind you and around you, felt but unseen, you sense the presence of the Guardians of this Circle and its Powers, Guardians of all it contains and all it connects. These are the Sidhe, and they welcome you into this place and their presence. Take a moment to go deeply into the felt sense of their ancient lineage of protecting and caring for the Life and Presence of Circles like this one and through them the life of the world.

You are now asked, "Will you share this Guardianship with us? Will you take on the Mantle we have worn? Will you be part of the Lineage that guards the thresholds, opens the Cauldrons of loving spirit, and releases new Life into the World? Will you be an agent of wholeness in the world?"

Take a moment to feel deeply and fully into what is being asked of you and what you think its implications may be for you personally in your life. How will you stand in this Lineage, wear this Mantle, and be a living Circle, Cauldron, or Grail in your world? When you feel ready, you can say "Yes" or "No."

A "No" will not disconnect you from the Sidhe in any way nor be a mark against you. It is simply a statement that you feel this is not your path or that the timing is not right, or you don't fully understand what a Yes might mean or bring. A No is a statement of your sovereignty and is fully honored and blessed by the Sidhe. If you do say "No," then receive the blessing of the unseen Guardians and step out of the Stone Circle. You can always reenter at another time that may be more appropriate.

If you have said "No," take a moment to stand in your Sovereignty, and then go about your business in your everyday world. The exercise is ended.

If you say "Yes," then take a moment of silence standing in the Circle among the Guardians, of whom you are now one. Be attentive in a calm way to anything that may occur or pass between the Sidhe and you.

You have always been a Power of love and holding in the world and a threshold between the worlds. You have always been a Grail. Taking on the mantle of Guardianship which the Sidhe have offered only adds to what you already are, affirming it, anchoring it, giving it a new flavor and potential. Just what this means is what you will discover in your own unique way.

At this point, the stones in the Circle begin to shimmer with Light. They dissolve and flow joyously and easily into your heart. Take a moment to feel the presence of the Circle shining within your being, your life, your heart. You ARE the Circle, the Portal, the Cauldron, the Grail.

You have always been these things, but now you engage with them in a new way that will unfold in the days and months and years ahead.

If you have the Sidhe Card Deck, now is the time to lay out a Stone Circle with the Howe in the middle. As you do so, see yourself externalizing the power of the Circle into your life and world. The Stone Circle has transmigrated from the Land to your Life. You are a Guardian of its power and presence within your life. [If you do not have a Sidhe Card Deck, simply imagine Standing Stones flowing out from your heart to take shape around you.] Take a moment to stand in the midst of the Circle of your own Life and feel what it means to you.

Now, with gratefulness to the Sidhe, to your own Sacredness, to Gaia, and to the Sacredness within all things, bring this exercise to a close. Stand in your sovereignty for a moment, and then go about your everyday business as a Circle of Light in your world.

If you feel the Sidhe show up while you're doing this exercise, then go with that experience. However, the objective of this exercise isn't to contact the Sidhe. It's really to contact that part of your own humanity that is Sidhe-like. It's an exercise in taking on the kind of responsibility towards the world and its life that the Sidhe carry and in the process, building an affinity with them.

STORIES

When I was putting together this book of new conversations with Mariel, I thought it would be important to include stories from people whom I know who are already making their own contacts with the Sidhe to illustrate both its possibility and some of the diverse forms it can take. Here are some of the stories I received.

Jeremy Berg

I have described some of my encounters with the Sidhe in art and story form in David Spangler's and my *Card Deck of the Sidhe* and also in my books *Faerie Blood* and *A Knight to Remember: Visions with the Sidhe*. It has been my experience that there are distinct groups of Sidhe who seem to me to have different interests, tasks, organization and connection to locals. One encounter which stands out to me is from a trip to Northern Scotland. My wife Freya and I were attending the "New Story Conference" put on by the Findhorn Community. I had met the local Sidhe on an earlier trip where they had helped me prepare a talk to the community on the Sidhe. This Scottish group always seems clannish to me and have a dry sense of humor. When I thanked them for their help with my talk they commented, "Well, we always do what the Star Priestess asks." This I took to refer to Mariel and while the comment was not really begrudging it was accompanied by a wry chuckle that their arms had been twisted a bit to assist.

It is easy to conceive of the Sidhe as some exotic species untainted by down to earth concerns. But, my story following belies that idea.

During the conference I asked the group of Sidhe I had met previously to help hold the space in which the activities were taking place. This they seemed to do as the week progressed. In attendance as a presenter at the conference was a wonderful Namibian woman who lead several ceremonies designed to balance male and female energies. In one such ritual she had male attendees meet individual women at the center of a large hall. The woman would hand a string with pine cones attached to the man and the man would tie it around her waist or head depending on the woman's age. Since there were dozens more women in the ritual than men we cycled around several times. All went smoothly for two rounds and the ceremony felt healing for both the men and women. However, while I was standing in the queue a voice said, "You will need to show up shortly". When I met a third young woman at the center she snapped the string away when I reached for it and began screaming and howling at me. This she did for several minutes while I tried to convey through body language that it was alright and that she could download her pain to me. After a while, though, I noticed a slight lull in the storm and a small smirk on her face. I stood from my kneeling position and began screaming and howling right back to her and we stood doing that for a few minutes until both of us began laughing. She then handed me the string and I tied the knot and we went offstage refreshed.

The Sidhe's comment, "Hmmm .... it appears you have a pair. I guess you can stand with us."

Claire Blatchford

Early in December I went outdoors to gather mosses for an Advent arrangement. As I stepped off the road and into the woods I was greeted by a strong, clear voice asking, "Where have you been?"

I knew, as I heard this voice within, it was Talus, a Sidhe neighbor, whom I first connected with about six years ago. Since then we've had occasional walks, talks and visits. Talus has visited briefly in our home. He has also, to my surprise, joined me at concerts and informed me of the importance to the Sidhe of certain kinds of music.

When we talk together what do we talk about? How to walk the blessing walk which, on a given day, may mean being alert to friendships among trees, rocks and rivers; the watchful presence in our area of Native Americans; the beings besides fish that live in our rivers; not allowing discontent to obscure or dull one's vision; learning to look and listen for harmony beneath discord, and, through such looking and listening, drawing harmony out.

The conversation is not entirely one way. Talus has questions for me. And I can feel his puzzlements.

"Where have you been?"

There was nothing accusatory in the greeting, but I felt it immediately and directly in my heart.

What he was saying was, "Welcome back! I'm *so* glad to be with you again!"

Where had I been?

I'd been completely caught up in the presidential election. How could I begin to explain *that* to him? How could I begin to look and listen for harmony in *that*? Just being with him again presented the challenge to get going on that!

Christy Carl

I walked in our woods and was near the small grove of very large trees, a couple of cedars and a hemlock whose roots intertwine. Years ago, they identified themselves as the Sidhe Trees. I often sense the Sidhe presence there, although usually my connection with a Sidhe person is during a meditation time. Anyway, today a Sidhe collective-type voice spoke when I was near these trees and said, "We live here with you (meaning Ron and me) to assist you with your work on this land."

With this, I realized that the Sidhe presence is one of the reasons I was led to this land. I know Ron has much more personal and frequent connection with Sidhe people. Mine tend to be a message here and a message there such as this one and the time they asked me to have Jeremy Berg come and hold a "connecting with the Sidhe" workshop.

Søren Hauge

I have had the privilege to conduct many Sidhe-workshops during the last four years, mainly in Denmark. These activities and the writing of four Sidhe-related books (one of them being *The Wild Alliance*, published by Lorian Press) has been the creative output stemming from a Sidhe companion I know as Fjeldur. The relationship is one of mutual inspiration and partnership focused on a shared interest in reviving our ancient Gaian heritage and weaving it into our modern world. Fjeldur is a singer and a shaman in his own world and I am a lover of the poetic language and a teacher in my world. We share a love for the Nordic identity and landscapes and its possible gifts to the world. Rooted in the land in our different ways, we have agreed to experiment and see what may come out of such a mutuality.

Here is how my engagement with the Sidhe and my contact with Fjeldur came about.

My first conscious recognition of the Sidhe Realm was a general sensing of a deep, nature-related field of humanoid presence with a touch of melancholy. It was different from the experiences I had earlier had with the Angelic or Nature Spirit realm – more closely related to the Human realm, yet part of nature and with a fluidity not typically human. It was like sensing a landscape parallel to the human and angelic. I was deeply touched. Thanks to the teachings from David and the sharing in a Lorian forum, I could now differentiate what I had earlier suspected was devic or angelic. From this touch unfolded a general 'feeling' of this deeply rooted world as part of the Gaian wholeness – a growing intimacy of getting acquainted with a new, large room in the vast house of life. I felt a mixture of magical presence, wonder and ancient memory surfacing in my conscious life. It was deeply touching, like rediscovering something lost and long forgotten.

As I endeavored to share with other people in workshops the Sidhe realm and the importance of renewed cooperation, something changed. Gradually, I felt a specific presence drawing nearer. Some of the participants in the workshops also sensed it, but I didn't want to create a focus on it, so I kept it as a gentle space I invited and cherished.

During one two-day workshop, in the interval between the two days, I felt I had to attune to this gentle and yet powerful presence. It was as if I leaned into a clear intention, and soon I was writing a message of erect dignity and wild wind, inviting the participants to a new journey. I also wrote 'Fjeldur' – but the word was omitted as I did not know what to do with it. The next day, I shared this written intention with the participants, and it was warmly received.

Months later, I found the word Fjeldur again. I had avoided it, but now it was obvious. It was a signature from the presence I was learning to recognize, and I suddenly 'knew' that it meant 'a mountain full of music'. It was a lyrical name with a distinct, Nordic tone. My thoughts went to Iceland and the Faroe Islands. Later I found out that there are many similar Faroese words, but none are identical. Icelandic and Faroese languages are closest to the language of the ancient Nordic countries, including Norway, Sweden, Denmark and Finland, in addition to Iceland and the Faroe Islands. And yet – the word Fjeldur was a musical poem in its own right, an expression of the being I was learning to know.

Following this there was a growing ability for me to recognize this 'Fjeldurian' presence. I could sense this atmosphere in a similar way that I can 'feel' the presence of a friend or relative without seeing them with my eyes. It was a growing intimacy. It was a distinct male presence, and

I was allowed to call him Fjeldur. It was a journey of coming together in an intimate, yet new relationship. Familiarity opened for affection from my side, and it was answered with a deep intention, opening as an invitation to shared cooperation. Very early he let me know that he was deeply connected to the Nordic region, and he would like to participate in a journey of discovering the gifts of the North.

In the following months and years, I sometimes received vivid, visual impressions when he approached me. His gentle, masculine presence was full of the mountainsides of the Nordic countries and the grass-filled highlands with smells of flowers and the touch of the wind. I had a felt sense of heather, moss, pine or fir trees, resin, mountains, topsoil and honey. I felt the blowing wind and sometimes antlers. At other times, I felt him as a huge hummingbird or a gigantic honey bee when he was approaching, calibrating to my presence. He carries with him the scents of the North, coupled with a deep, poetic joy, a lyrical depth and a deep affinity for the energy of the land that makes me sing and dance. And as the journey has unfolded into many workshops and several books, it is as if our minds can lean into each other. The visual sensing is lessened – perhaps because less energy is needed for the contact. Today I truly feel that he is a friend and a colleague, and that we are partners on a journey of bridging worlds. It is a shamanic, co-creative journey bringing fruits of the past into a seeding of the Gaian future of wholeness.

The effects of the contact have been numerous. Of course, the inspiration that has enriched my books and workshops has been remarkable. Besides this, I can sense a clear and distinct effect in my love of dancing to music and in incorporating movements in simple, improvised rituals. There is a new element of spontaneous awareness and a new exploration into wildness and exploring the "in-between" in life. I have also noticed that when I have asked for help, the response has been surprisingly quick and notable, as if there are special hotlines between the Sidhe-realm and our world. I am also aware that Fjeldur's presence has helped to set free my ability to write much more poetically than I allowed myself to do earlier. In the same way, I feel that his connection with me enriches his ability to engage with humans, and I have a feeling that he is sharing this in his realm.

Ron Hays

The Gates - Sidhe Card Deck

I use the images of the Sidhe card deck to connect with the Sidhe realm. Standing outdoors on our land, I visualize the Earth Gate at my feet, the Star Gate above my head, the Gate of Dawn to the East, and Twilight Gate to the West. Each Gate fills me with its unique vibratory quality. If the felt sense of the Heart Stones—Wizard, Artisan, Bard, and Gateway—arises in me, my connection progresses. Otherwise I drop the attempt. If the link strengthens, I sense being drawn deeper into connection with the Sidhe and the possibility of a collaborative communication.

(Wood)-Working with the Sidhe

In my woodworking business, *Elven Gates*, I build large outdoor wooden portals. As I fabricate one of these gates, I collaborate with the Sidhe on my projects. I do so by sharing a visualization of my concept of object with them. Often, I receive feedback. For example, I wanted to attach two adjacent pieces of wood with a metal fastener. But in "conversation" with them I sensed that the free flow of energy would be disrupted by a screw or bolt and the vibratory quality of the piece would be diminished. I "heard" that I should reconsider how to join the parts. By changing methods I made a more refined and aesthetically pleasing portal.

Two large sections of another gate needed connecting after fabrication. I believed some form of metal fastener was required. Not wanting to interrupt the energetic connection between the parts, I brought my concerns to my Sidhe colleagues. They seemed unconcerned about a metal fastener, but I heard "We'll sleep on it and get back to you." A couple of days later I connected back in and felt this thrill of energy from them. An image formed in my mind of two hands, palm to palm, fingers pointing upwards. These hands were made of brass and attached to the top of each section. The hands then were bolted together to join each half of the portal. In this collaborative process, the Sidhe provided me with an energetic impulse that enabled the image of the hands to arise in my mind.

Visiting the Sidhe

My recent explorations are leading me to explore the similarities and differences between our physical world and the non-physical dimension of the Sidhe. Both have a form of materiality. But in their realm the formation of "structures" requires an attunement to and weaving together of various vibratory patterns and energies. Just as building a quality house in the physical realm requires a master builder, constructing a Sidhe "home" requires mastery of and experience with their "matter".

I work with a group a Sidhe in a "local" village. In my "visits" there I am enveloped in a sense of the neighborliness, warmth, and community that they share. I know no individuals by name but I often encounter a couple with a young child. On several occasions the child has offered me a "gift". Accepting these "gifts" I'm filled with a profound sense of safety, well being, or peace.

In a recent visit to the Sidhe village I was asking why they had homes when they do not contend with the elements--there's no need to keep the rain off their heads. In response they invited me into one of their homes. When I went in, my sense was of crossing into a pillowy softness filled with warmth and family. A place that contained privacy and wellbeing. All the qualities that we associate with being at home.

A few days later I was invited to "dinner" at one of their houses. I understand that Sidhe "food" is vibratory. A quality we often fail to consider in consuming our physical food. I was asked to bring something for "dinner". That stopped me. What could I possibly bring? It occurred to me to bring the quality of nature that I experienced during my prior walk. Their response was quite positive. Then recalling that I was fretting about something while walking, I hesitated and explained that it might not be a good idea to bring my nature experience after all. Their response was: "Oh don't worry about that we'll just "wash" it off the way you wash the dirt off carrots plucked from the ground."

Lucinda Herring

The Card Deck of the Sidhe rests on my altar, beneath a larger print of the Howe. I create the Stone Circle almost every day, something I have never done with a deck of cards before. This is because they are not just a deck. Over time, with intentional use, the cards have become a portable living portal – a kind of way station or commons where I can go to commune with the Sidhe. It's hard to describe, but the stones on the cards are completely real to me now. I put the Gate of Earth down first, and immediately I am transported to a place where that dolmen is real. I reach out my hand, and I can feel the living texture of the huge stones, down to the lichen growing between the cracks, and the warm sun beating down on my face. And this is true for every stone in the circle. My felt sense of each is so vivid and visceral, it still takes my breath away. I make my way round the circle, and greet each stone as a beloved friend. Depending on what I am feeling and thinking that day, I might stop and commune with one or another for longer than usual – read the manual for that particular stone, draw a Dancer card, or simply rest and listen. Eventually I find myself at the entrance to the Howe. I don't always go in. Some days I just call out a greeting, and link up with the Sidhe in my heart. Other days I enter, light a candle and make my way to a glyph doorway carved on a back wall deep within. I open that doorway, and then I wait. Sometime my call is answered.

I never see my Sidhe companions. I just feel them draw near. My senses become heightened, and I at times feel swirls of energy around me. I have come to know some individuals as a specific gesture or movement in the field, sometimes a familiar imagery, though I doubt that's what they really look like. For the past year now, I often make my way across a meadow to a beautiful pool or well of stars, something I simply discovered one day in my wanderings. I have been guided to dive into that pool, and swim in the quiet depths of starlight. Doing so is deeply cleansing and restorative. I feel completely happy there. If I wake depressed or out of sorts, I only have to do this to gather myself again and face the day. One day last summer, when I stepped out of the pool, I was wearing a cloak of stars that fit my body like a membrane or second skin. And a crystal blue star rested on my forehead as a talisman. I was told these were gifts, ones that could help me in my work. They are a living permeable boundary - serving both as protection and connection with the Sidhe, I believe. I am still exploring these treasures, and no doubt will do so for a long time to come. I am grateful.

I am a writer and Lorian minister, and I care for the dead and their grieving families and friends. I have learned to call on my Sidhe companions in my work. They are tangibly helpful in keeping me grounded within the often chaotic and mysterious threshold of death. I know I must be grounded in my own body for them to draw near, and this intention to focus on the physical serves me well in those shifting times. The Sidhe seem quite interested in how we humans die, and in our emotions and deep feelings of sorrow and loss at losing our physical forms. I have asked the Sidhe to be present with me when I need to hold huge gatherings of shocked and grieving people. Twice, I have had to create memorial services and write the eulogies of people who have died, even though I never knew those people in life. I believe the Sidhe have aided me in contacting those people in the post-mortem realms in safe and effective ways, so that I could truly tell their stories. I feel my capacity to be in my sovereignty and power while I am communicating has been strengthened in working with the Sidhe – they enhance my Bardic self, as writer, storyteller and speaker. In return, I invite my Sidhe friends into my daily life, whenever I can remember, as they seem fascinated with our world of matter and more rigid form. I invite them to see through my eyes, explore through my hands and body, experience the richness of what it means to be a human. Especially a human who is delighted to engage with her long-lost cousins once again!

Mary Inglis

From time to time I invite the Sidhe to 'see' and engage with the world through the portal of my awareness and presence. When I do this, it feels to me that there's a merging of perspective to create a kind of joint awareness – so while they may be seeing through my eyes, at the same time, because of this, I begin seeing things differently or newly as well, as if seeing through their eyes and awareness. I become aware of how I am part of a living and interconnected environment in which everything I look at seems to become more itself, more vibrant and alive.

While doing Jeremy's class 'At Home with the Sidhe' in 2016, I invited any interested Sidhe to join me while driving one day. One of the things that caught my attention was the car, and I had the sense that whoever was present with me was interested in this, so I began talking about it, explaining what the different things were for (steering wheel, brakes, indicators, windscreen wipers, gear shift, etc.), while imagining someone sitting next to me in the passenger seat (and indeed, I increasingly began to have a sense of a presence there). Then I found my/our attention going to the engine. This is not something I generally think about; I take it for granted. But this time I found myself marveling at the human creativity and ingenuity that has created the internal combustion engine... and all the other elements that make up a functioning car. And also how much time and how many incremental steps have gone into the creation and development of that engine, and into all its many uses, and into the creation not just of cars but also the particular car we were occupying at that moment.

I felt it was not just my awareness that was marveling at this, but also the Sidhe awareness. And that this creation step-by-step over time was something that was registering and interesting for both of us. I also felt that my companion had quite a lot of curiosity about how the internal combustion engine works, but I had to tell him or her that I actually had very little idea about this.

Later I was sharing this experience with a friend and she began laughing. I am not known for my interest in internal combustion engines, and the idea of someone coming to me for information about them is somewhat ludicrous. However, she had also suddenly had this picture of a Sidhe person returning to her or his class on 'Coming Home to the Humans', and excitedly sharing about their connection with this human who had told them all about cars and the internal combustion engine.

She was reminded of something David said at one point about needing to be careful about giving too much weight to communications or messages from non-physical beings... if Uncle Fred was an idiot when he was alive on earth, he was unlikely to have suddenly become all-wise and all-knowledgeable in the post-mortem realms (I don't know that David said it exactly like this).

Hopefully my friend wasn't calling me an idiot, but it is certainly true that I am no authority on the workings of engines. Just as we may need to be careful about giving too much weight to communications from beings who don't occupy our level of existence, so they too may need to be careful about giving too much weight to communications from us. (I'm not sure 'communication' is the right word, at least not in the form of messages, because the information arises of out the experience of a shared collaborative field in the moment.)

In the programs I run, I quite often invite the presence and engagement of any interested Sidhe. I notice that this often seems to result in a heightened energy, something enlivening and alert. It creates a sense of a cohesive and collaborative learning field in which a lot of synchronicities happen and what feel to be deeper and more profound learnings occur. One of the approaches I use in my work is learning about something or an experience by taking the shape of that thing, going into the subjective experience of it and learning about it from the inside. As shape-shifting is one of the attributes of the Sidhe, it feels like this is a point of resonance that is a portal of connection as well as maybe something interesting to them, and something we can engage with together. The sense of a heightened, often sparkly, collective field seems confirmation of this.

Geoff Oelsner

(The following stories are from Geoff's book, *A Country Where All Colors Are Sacred and Alive*, published in 2012, Lorian Press, used with his permission and suggestion.)

The Old Ones (1975)

Like many individuals before me over the centuries, I've sensed beings from a parallel realm while visiting certain places in the U.K., and the U.S. Known by many names, including the "faery folk" or the "Sidhe" in Ireland and Scotland, these beings seem to be quite different from the more diminutive, gossamer fairies of familiar fairy tales. However, the dissimilar spellings can be confusing, because these two words are frequently used interchangeably to denote both the small, aerial flower fairies and the more formidable, subterranean Sidhe. In this book, the word "fairy" is used to specify the former and "faery" the latter beings. If my intuitions are at all accurate, the faery folk are powerful, watchful, exalted and often wise. I wonder how one of them would characterize us humans? The following poems are descriptive reports, and gestures of connection made to an ancient race:

Glimpses of Faeryland

We check in at a bed and breakfast near Mellaray Abbey, below the Knocknealdown Mountains of southern Ireland.

After sinking into the first deep waters of sleep, I return to my identity. I'm standing on an immense gloomy stone stairway, surrounded by mossy walls of unseen height. I have no idea where my sleeping body lies, I'm so carried away, into a realm as real as this waking one and more, for in my translocation this seems to be the only moment that has ever been.

Now I'm drawn down the stairs through a percipient, not-unfriendly darkness and suddenly come upon a marvelous city of silver domed dwellings with intricate curlicues and designs upon them. Silver horns and moons curve upward from the roofs.

This is certainly not my place. I find it very difficult to return to form. After a minute or so of trying, I have to call on my spiritual protectors to draw me bodyward again. Passing through a conflagration of great winds, I fly up the tunnel back to our bed and breakfast room where my napping body lies, and slowly lower down into my flesh. Years later, I read in a book of Irish lore that the underground Hall of the Queen of the Faeries is said to be located at the foot of the Knocknealdown Mountains, precisely the site of that bed and breakfast place. In retrospect, I think I may have glimpsed the fabled "faery city under the mountain," as convincing as our own reality, yet so conclusively OTHER.

The Faery Feather (2011)

June sun presses its big hot thumb down on the concrete parking lot as I arrive at the Ozark Natural Foods Cooperative in Fayetteville, and back into a parking slot at the very edge of the shopping center. As I lock my car, I happen to see a large feather just behind it in a narrow perimeter area strewn with trash and tough, scrawny plants. Not wanting to unlock the car doors again, I pick the feather up and slip it through an open window. It wafts down to the front seat. I go into the co-op and shop, then head back toward my car with a bag of groceries. As I get about eight feet from my car, to my utter astonishment, the front door on the driver's side suddenly swings open, pauses for a moment as if to be witnessed, then closes itself firmly.

I reach the car, and try the door. It's locked!

I take the feather home, and place it on my altar, and later cleanse it with Peruvian *palo santo* wood, in much the same way that some people burn dried sage, sweetgrass, cedar, or juniper to "smudge" and purify a room, an object, or themselves. Later still at twilight, I fit the feather into the slit end of a long wand of sycamore that's been stripped of bark and neatly gnawed by a beaver at the King's River.

Among animals, I feel a kinship with the Beaver Clan. Thus the beaver stick. The great Seneca medicine woman Twylah Nitsch once told me that in her tribe I'd be numbered among members of the Beaver Clan, because one of my keynotes is cooperation, embodied by beavers who build their dams together and live in colonies of nuclear family units, each family residing in its own lodge. Brandishing that fine-feathered beaver stick, I dance and celebrate the mystery of life and all its hidden kingdoms in the deep purple half-dark of dusk.

I wonder whether this mind-boggling event at the co-op has anything to do with earlier dreams and visions, and other more recent experiences with rings and buttons and sightings of small lights which have happened with some frequency in the first months of 2011. As I look back on these incidents, I ponder possible tie-ins with experiences I had in the nineteen seventies in Britain, and while making recent attunements in order to build collaborative relationships with local Nature spirits, and with the beings known to the Irish and the Scottish as the Sidhe, the ancient, evolved faery folk.

Just before the door-which-opened-and-closed itself, I'd become curious about the Sidhe. After reading the Celtic scholar John Matthews' account of his purported meetings with a representative of that distinguished line of subtle beings in *The Sidhe: Wisdom from the Celtic Otherworld*, I wanted to learn more about the history of human-faery interactions. In the days just prior to the enigmatic event at the co-op, I read a number of books that contain accounts by other supposed contactees, such as the Reverend Robert Kirk's extraordinary manuscript from the late 1600's, *The Secret Commonwealth of Elves, Fauns and Faeries*; W.Y. Evans-Wentz's huge, absorbing ethnographic collection of sightings, *The Fairy Faith in Celtic Countries*; selected books and essays by William Butler Yeats and his mystic Irish contemporary George Russell (aka A.E.); Eddie Lenihan's remarkable collection of recent faery sightings and interactions with humans in Ireland, *Meeting the Other Crowd*; and books by other modern authors who profess to have experience of the faery realm, including American author and mage Orion Foxwood, the spiritually gifted Scot R.J. Stewart, William Bloom, Brian Froud, and Signe Pike.

Perhaps all this reading opened me to a contact of my own, or at the least disposed me to a florid act of the imagination. At any rate, looking back now and connecting the dots... the very night before my weird experience in the parking lot, as I lie down to go to sleep, a rapturous, tingly feeling comes over me. It's so pleasant, I exclaim out loud, "I feel sooooo good," then rest back into a vibrant sense of well-being. The next thing I know, I feel a distinct presence enter my energy field and gently merge with my body awareness.

What I sense is friendly, but very Other, with both plantlike and human attributes; katydid green, greenleaf green, humming with life and brightly energized. For a minute more or less I feel doubled--a juxtaposition of myself and an uplifting yet serious masculine entity which seems like a diplomatic emissary from some parallel dimension of this Earth. Wonderment...

The next morning, when my car door swings open and closed at the co-op, I begin to suspect that the reverie of the previous night, and other earlier tokens of connection (such as finding the little button on my bathroom floor) might have been related, and led up to the moment when that door swung open, really grabbing my attention and confirming a genuine contact.

I am aware of our anthropomorphic tendency to personify subtle forces. Many people would be more comfortable with the notion that one might encounter energies, rather than actual entities of Nature. However, many others have reported sighting or sensing Nature spirits which seem to present themselves as described in venerable myths, or to mimic human behaviors, apparel, and habitations. This may be due solely to our own human projections, but it is also possible that these sentient energies "clothe" themselves in familiar forms for the sake of connecting with us in ways which we can relate to.

A day or two after the event at the co-op, a further synchronicity echoes and affirms my own experiences: I receive a journal in the mail from David Spangler [*Views from the Borderland*, available by subscription from the Lorian Association] in which he describes an unexpected contact he feels he has made quite recently with a member of the Sidhe. In his article, David writes:

"The contact with the Sidhe... has opened up new ways of thinking about the challenges that humanity is facing, and the help we are receiving... Contact with the Sidhe can be exciting for its own sake, but the deeper purpose behind what appears to be a new approach towards reconciliation is to break through the bubble that is forming around humanity due to the increasingly self-referential and humancentric attitudes and behaviors that characterize industrial and technological society... In this sense, the Sidhe become exemplars for us but not with the purpose of surrounding us with glamour or turning us away from our humanity. Rather it is to discover the larger, fuller humanity that can embrace both Sidhe and human beings and bring both into a new collaborative relationship. We need to break out of the human-centric bubble but not in a way that destroys or disperses our humanity. Paradoxically, the Sidhe, by mirroring what a Gaian humanity might be like, can help us accomplish this."

Susan Sherman

The Sidhe and Healing

Several years ago, I had given my two-week notice working as a paralegal. I was looking forward to leaving the legal field behind me, and jumping head first into learning all about the health benefits of organic teas and the business nuances of a biodynamic tea farm. I needed a break, and one week into my notice period, I fell off our deck. Three pelvic fractures, a sacrum fracture and significant pain landed me a three-day hospital stay. Unfortunately, this was not the break I had had in mind. The upside, however, was that I had wonderful nursing care, rested deeply, and enjoyed the peaceful view outside my room. Three weeks later with walker in hand, my husband and I made our annual sojourn to the Seattle area for a Lorian gathering. What we discovered is that traveling with a walker or wheelchair has certain benefits, and we were escorted through the busy airports with ease. This is how I arrived in Seattle - pushing my walker and taking it slowly.

The weekend was rich with deep discussions, inner practice, comradery and good food. For our last inner working of the Lorian gathering weekend, David guided the group in a Gaian journey. As we focused on the Gaian pool and the memory of the sun, moon and stars embodied within the pool, I found myself absorbing the myriad of energies into my body. I remember being in the meadow, and standing in a circle, and the incredible Light - and then I was gone and I really do not remember the rest of what was said except for being brought back to circle, and the powerful Love that encircled us all as we held hands. The Love was so very palpable and the group felt so strong, purposeful, grounded and joyful. It felt (and continues to feel) that our commitment to the work with Gaia deepened to a new and more profound level.

After the weekend get together, on Monday my husband and our friend were talking about politics and I excused myself to another room to meditate. A recent copy of "Borderlands" lay on the end table, and I randomly opened it to the Guardian exercise, which invites a doorway to connect with the Sidhe. We had touched upon the Guardian exercise during the weekend - I began.

As I stepped into the ancient stone circle - "a great Cauldron held by Gaia" - with an awareness of the stars, moon, sun and deep earth, I felt an immersion and soaking in of these energies (or resonances) similar to the pool exercise we had practiced together on Sunday. This time, however, I was fully engaged. When I read these questions - "Will you share this Guardianship with us? Will you take on the Mantle we have worn? Will you be part of the Lineage that guards the thresholds, opens the Cauldrons of loving spirit, and releases new Life into the World?" - every part of my being resonated with a resounding *"Yes"*. The accompanying felt sense was an expansion of my inner self meeting this sacred commitment - one which I recognized from long ago and which even as I write now continues to resonate in my body and soul.

I found the final step of the working particularly empowering. It was simple appreciation - feelings of gratefulness and appreciation exuded from me - to the Sidhe, to Gaia, to my own Sacredness and particularly to the Sacredness within all things. This is where my true love lies - learning to recognize and enhance the awareness of the sacredness of all things. The sense of being a Circle of Light in my everyday world felt natural - of course, this is me, and I bless and care and love. And, I remembered that several times while in the hospital and since, I have felt the presence of a feminine being holding space with me, and I resolved to deepen that connection and partnership.

As I finished meditating, I opened my eyes and stood, reaching my fingertips out and lovingly and gently touched the wall which felt to be an intricate part of this experience - holding me - an exchange of love so deep was present. Our friends' wedding picture was on the wall next to a photo of their son, and I was moved to touch each of the pictures and could feel the flow of love between myself and each of them. And then I walked... without walker, without pain or awkward gait... freely and whole. I was left with the impression that it is not that we heal "into" wholeness (which to me carries a sense of being separated in moving from illness/disease/pain <u>to</u> wholeness), but that we heal "through" our wholeness. This is what I experienced.

Needless to say, my husband and our friend were quite surprised when out I walked into the living room without the walker! I did my best to share the experience with them through tears of joy and words of love - it was truly a lovely experience and one I wanted to share with them because this inner work is so very important to our future and has been to me personally.

I am deeply grateful for David and for the work he has done and continues to do and for the hope that humanity and Gaia will partner more fully in sacredness.

And so, the physical manifestation piece is that I walked freely without any pain for over six hours. Since that Guardian day with the Sidhe, and after flying the redeye back to Traverse City, x-rays taken again, the fractures had healed extremely well, and I was discharged from PT. So, all is well!

I've had a sticky note on my computer for a few weeks now. It reads - "Find that place... where your deep gladness and the world's deep hunger meet." I believe I have found a doorway to that place and feel very blessed.

Blessings to all who have the honor to read David's book, blessings to the Sidhe, to Gaia and to the Work.

These stories give some flavor of what it can mean to be in contact with the Sidhe. The important thing is to realize how individual it all is. Like any relationship, the engagement is shaped by the people involved, their interests, needs, characteristics, and so on. Mariel may speak generally about how the Sidhe engage humanity, but in practice, it is with individuals, both human and Sidhe, that this manifests. What may work for one person may not work for another.

I believe an essential element for such human and Sidhe relationships is ordinariness. Keeping it ordinary and normal. Glamor just gets in the way, as it does in human to human relationships. We may look for dramatic occurrences, but the interaction may be very simple. Sometimes the simplest way to start is to invite a Sidhe to look through your eyes as you go about your day and to see your world as you see it. This can be as exciting and mysterious to them as seeing their world would be to us.

However it may manifest, relationship with the Sidhe is not a far-fetched or fanciful idea. Many people are having the experience. I believe many more will join them in the months and years ahead.

FINAL THOUGHTS

I feel it's important to state the obvious: I am only one person having conversations with a single Sidhe. While they give me insights, they certainly don't make me an expert on the Sidhe.

Looking back over these conversations, I believe I have shared Mariel's thoughts as accurately as I could, though there were times when it was not easy to fully grasp the concepts she was presenting. As she often says, her world and way of thinking and being are different from ours. However, I'm keenly aware of what is left out, of what I could not capture in my words.

I know Mariel shares some of my frustration in this regard. As she says more than once, her world is very different from ours. It's just as complex and rich in its own way, but because it is different, it doesn't reduce easily to familiar human images. I talk about her mountain, her forests, her city, her village, and so on, but these are human labels placed on phenomena that are beyond my ability to describe. They really aren't like a city or a forest as we would experience these things, and yet, they are, in function and beauty if not always in appearance. Part of the challenge, as I wrote earlier, is that Mariel's world exists simultaneously on several levels of being. One of her trees is so much more complex in manifestation than the trees we see in our environments, but it is still a tree, so that's what I call it. In putting it into my human imagery and language, though, it's like straining a rich stew through a filter that leaves only a pale, thin broth at the end.

One thing I also wish I could convey in its fullness but lack the words to do so is Mariel's presence, in particular, her joy and her sense of humor. She laughs often.

If the contact between us is mainly telepathic, then all I receive are her thoughts in response to my questions. In a way, it's like reading a telegraph. But if we are "being-melding," I am very aware of being held in a presence that is light, effervescent, and joyous, even when discussing serious matters. It's that presence I wish to highlight. The gift of her and her people, as she said, is that of a joyous presence—not necessarily what we would think of as a "happy" one but one that enhances life in an exuberance and exhilaration of being alive and part of a living, interconnected universe.

Most of these conversations have taken place during a challenging time in the United States where I live. The election and inauguration of Donald Trump as President has generated conflict, hope, despair, anger, and fear, emotions not at all confined to the United States but certainly heightened for those of us living here. It doesn't matter what a person's political philosophy or affiliation is; at the moment, the subtle environment reverberates to these emotions. This has at times made connection with Mariel difficult. It's exactly as if a windstorm has come up, making standing upright difficult and threatening to blow one over. Conversations were at times interrupted as one or the other of us had to withdraw to take time to center and stand in our inner centers of calm; often it was me who needed to deal with the pressures of the subtle environment before I could continue.

Yet during all this, I have felt a conviction that, in spite of how it looks on the surface, behind the scenes, in the realms of spirit, all is proceeding as it should and that a way is being cleared for a new birth of hope and vision within humanity. When I mentioned this to Mariel, she agreed and offered the following:

> **MARIEL**: There are those beings who see from the heights, as it were; their vision tells us that we are on a path together that will bring us ever closer towards wholeness. We, on the other hand, see as if from within the earth, for we are part of Gaia's body, part of the imagination of her life, as I have said. From our perspective, we see not what is there in the future but what is arising in the present, emerging from the world itself. Yes, there is turmoil, and much that is old and decaying is being forced to surface and show itself. It is not pleasant. But we see the Light of the world also emerging; we see it's joyous heart unfolding. We see human hearts and minds opening. We see compassion arising. It is a challenging time, but it is one filled with hope as well. We are not here to suffer an ending but to celebrate a beginning. It is one we can create together.
>
> I give you my blessings.

About the Publisher

Lorian Press LLC is a private, for profit business which publishes works approved by the Lorian Association. Current titles by David Spangler and others can be found on the Lorian website www.lorian.org.

The Lorian Association is a not-for-profit educational organization. Its work is to help people bring the joy, healing, and blessing of their personal spirituality into their everyday lives. This spirituality unfolds out of their unique lives and relationships to Spirit, by whatever name or in whatever form that Spirit is recognized. For more information, go to www.lorian.org.

www.ingramcontent.com/pod-product-compliance
Lightning Source LLC
Chambersburg PA
CBHW021012090426
42738CB00007B/763